THE
SMARTYPANTS'

GUIDE
TO THE
AP ENVIRONMENTAL SCIENCE EXAM

Michelle Mahanian

Smartypants Publishing ™

Smartypants Publishing
www.smartypantsguides.com
Email: booksupport@smartypantsguides.com

AP and Advanced Placement are registered trademarks of the College Entrance Examination Board, which was not involved in the production of, and does not endorse, this book.

Printed in the United States of America.

ISBN: 978-1-4116-4477-9

ACKNOWLEDGEMENTS

I would like to thank all of my former teachers and classmates at Palisades High School for giving me the knowledge, advice, and support to write this book, and especially, Mr. Brendhen Van Loo. His genuine love for teaching along with his warm heart, brilliant mind, and caring personality are what inspired my passion for science. Moreover, thanks to everyone in my loving family for always backing up my crazy dreams and motivating me to make them a reality. I would be nothing without your love and encouragement and I am so blessed to have you in my life.

- Michelle Mahanian

TABLE OF CONTENTS

PART I: INTRODUCTION

Format 3

Scoring 3

Breakdown by Topic 3

Approaching the Multiple-Choice Section 4

Approaching the Free-Response Section 5

How to Study for the AP Exam 7

The Day of the Exam 7

PART II: REVIEW OF KEY TOPICS

Energy Flow in Ecosystems Mon **11**

    Laws of Thermodynamics 11

    Photosynthesis 11

    Living Systems 12

    Food Chains and Food Webs 12

    Ecological Pyramids 13

Biogeochemical Cycles Mon **15**

    Water Cycle 15

    Carbon Cycle 15

    Nitrogen Cycle 16

    Phosphorus Cycle 16

    Sulfur Cycle 17

Biodiversity Mon **18**

    Theory of Evolution/Natural Selection 18

    Threats to Biodiversity 18

    Legislation Protecting Biodiversity 19

Species Interactions Tues **20**

    Predation 20

Competition and Territoriality 20

Symbiotic Relationships 21

Defense Mechanisms 21

Adapting to the Environment *Tues* **22**

Habitat and Niche 22

Law of Competitive Exclusion 22

Tolerance Range and Limiting Factors 23

Community Ecology *Tues* **24**

Keystone Species 24

Community Properties 24

Succession 25

Terrestrial Biomes *Tues* **26**

Deserts 26

Grasslands 26

Tundra 26

Coniferous Forests 27

Broad-leaved Deciduous Forests 27

Chaparral 27

Tropical Moist Forests 28

Aquatic Biomes *Wed* **29**

Freshwater 29

Marine 29

Wetlands 30

Restoration Ecology *Wed* **31**

Rehabilitation 31

Remediation 31

Reclamation and Re-creation 31

Overview of Population Dynamics *WED* **32**

Types of Growth 32

r-selected and K-selected Species 33

Survivorship Curves 33

Doubling Time 33

Human Overpopulation *WED* **34**

Important Factors 34

Perspectives on Overpopulation 34

The Developed and Developing Worlds 35

Age-Structure Histograms 35

Demographic Transition 36

Urbanization 37

Health and the Environment _TH_ **38**

Disease 38

Hazardous and Toxic Chemicals 38

DDT and Biomagnification 39

Ecological Economics _TH_ **40**

Economic Theory 40

Resources 40

Measuring Wealth and Quality of Life 41

Cost-Benefit Analysis 41

Organizations and Green Businesses 42

Environmental Policy and Law _TH_ **43**

NEPA 43

The Precautionary Principle 43

Land Use _TH_ **44**

Soil: Components and Horizons 44

Land Degradation 44

Sustainable Agriculture 45

Forests and Deforestation 46

Preserves and Wilderness Areas 47

The Arctic National Wildlife Refuge (ANWR) 47

Pest Control _FR_ **48**

Pesticide Benefits 48

Pesticide Problems 48

Alternatives to Using Pesticides 49

Regulation of Pesticides 49

Earth Science _FR_ **50**

Plate Tectonics 50

The Rock Cycle 50

Extracting Metals and Minerals 51

The Atmosphere and Global Climate *FR* **53**

    Atmospheric Layers 53

    Climate and Weather 54

    Global Warming and its Effects 55

Air Pollution *FR* **56**

    Air Pollutants and The Clean Air Act 56

    Controlling Air Pollution 57

    Impact of Air Pollution 59

Water Use *SA* **60**

    Sources of Water 60

    The Water Table 61

    Depleted Groundwater 61

    Environmental Impact of Dams 62

Water Pollution *SA* **63**

    Point and Nonpoint Sources 63

    Categories of Water Pollution 63

    The Clean Water Act 64

    Wastewater Treatment 65

Solid Waste *SA* **67**

    Disposal Methods 67

    Reducing Waste 68

    Hazardous and Toxic Wastes 69

Sources of Energy *Su* **70**

    Nonrenewable: Coal, Oil, and Natural Gas 70

    Nuclear Power 71

    Alternative Energy 72

    Conserving Energy 75

Environmental Disasters *Su* **76**

    Chernobyl, Ukraine 76

    Love Canal, New York 76

    Bhopal, India 76

    Three Mile Island, Pennsylvania 77

Important Individuals *Sun* **78**

Rachel Carson 78

Theodore Roosevelt and Gifford Pinchot 78

John Muir 78

Aldo Leopold 78

Environmental Laws and Agreements **79**

International Laws 79

National Laws 79

Index of Key Terms **81**

PART III: PRACTICE TEST

Practice Test 89

Grading Your Practice Test 107

Answer Key: Multiple-Choice 108

Explanations: Multiple-Choice 109

Free-Response Rubric 114

PART I:

INTRODUCTION

ABOUT THE AP EXAM

Format

Total Time: 3 hours

SECTION I: Multiple-Choice
Time – 90 minutes
Number of questions - 100
Percent of total grade – 60%

SECTION II: Free-Response
Time – 90 minutes
Number of questions – 4
Percent of total grade – 40%

Scoring

The AP Exam is graded on a scale from 1 to 5, with 5 corresponding to
"extremely well qualified" (best score) and 1 corresponding to "no
recommendation" (worst score). Most universities offer college credit for a score
of 3 or higher, which is considered passing. You should expect to get your AP
score in the mail by mid-July.

Breakdown by Topic

INTERDEPENDENCE OF EARTH'S SYSTEMS [25%] – includes evolution, the rock
cycle, the atmosphere, ecosystems, etc.

HUMAN POPULATION DYNAMICS [10%]

RENEWABLE AND NONRENEWABLE RESOURCES [15%]

ENVIRONMENTAL QUALITY [20-25%] – includes air/water/soil pollutants, impacts on human health, and solid waste.

GLOBAL CHANGES AND THEIR CONSEQUENCES [15-20%] – includes atmospheric changes, biodiversity loss, global warming, exotic species, etc.

ENVIRONMENT AND SOCIETY: TRADEOFFS AND DECISION-MAKING [10%] – includes economics, environmental laws, cultural and aesthetic considerations, and other issues.

Approaching the Multiple-Choice Section

1. Don't panic!
Think of the multiple-choice section as a game where you can make the most of the knowledge you've already acquired. Being nervous won't raise your score. Just focus on tackling the exam with the best strategy.

2. Make sure you understand the instructions.
Listen carefully as the proctor reads the instructions. If you don't understand something, raise your hand and clear it up before you begin the exam.

3. Keep an eye on the clock.
Remember: you will have only 90 minutes to answer 100 questions, each with five possible answers listed. You'll have a little less than a minute to answer each question and bubble in the correct answer choice. Don't spend too much time on any one question. If you can't figure something out, circle the question number in your booklet and come back to it if you have time.

4. If you finish early...
Go back to those questions you circled and try them again. Finally, take a good look at your answer sheet and double-check that you've bubbled in all of your answers on the correct line and that any erasure marks are completely gone.

This is important because the multiple-choice section is scored by a machine with no sympathy whatsoever!

5. **The guessing penalty shouldn't scare you. Use the process of elimination!**

In the multiple-choice section, one-fourth of the number of questions you answer incorrectly will be subtracted from the number of questions you answer correctly. This simply means that random guessing will not improve your score. Thus, if you can eliminate one or more answer choices, GUESS! You should be crossing off the answer choices you know are wrong until you are left with only one (correct) choice.

6. **No calculators allowed.**

This means that any problems that require math will use only basic calculations that you will be able to work out on paper. Don't get carried away!

Approaching the Free-Response Section

The free-response section includes one data-set question, one document-based question, and two synthesis and evaluation questions.

1. **Read the *entire* question before writing, and jot down notes on the side of the green booklet.**

You may want to write out a quick outline before you actually start writing. This will ensure that you answer all parts of the question.

2. **Write neatly! You don't want to put your reader in a bad mood!**

3. **If you're asked to design an experiment...**

Occasionally, a free-response question will ask you to design an experiment. If you find yourself in this situation, make sure you clearly define your hypothesis (educated guess), independent variable (what is being manipulated), dependent variable (what is being measured), and the control group (used for comparison).

Also, predict an outcome based on the data. Usually, this type of question has multiple parts (lettered a, b, c, etc), with each part asking you to explain a specific aspect of the experiment.

4. Time yourself.

You will have to answer four questions in 90 minutes, which means you'll have a little more than 20 minutes to answer each one. There are usually multiple parts to each free-response question. You don't necessarily have to go in order, so first do the ones you know best. That way, if you run out of time, you'll leave blank the questions you'd get wrong anyway.

5. The readers don't care about your essay-writing eloquence. Be clear and concise!

You don't need a thesis and topic sentences in the APES free-response; all you have to do is answer the question in a clear, organized, and straightforward manner. Try not to wander off topic; that will only waste your valuable time. You may also draw diagrams to clarify your point. Remember to label every part of the diagram.

6. Focus on the big picture, but throw in whatever facts you can remember.

The free-response section is graded with a rubric, so readers look for specific words or phrases in your answer. You won't lose points for the wrong information, so any facts you include can only earn you some extra points. Define any terms you use in your answer.

7. Don't give up!

At times during your 90-minute ordeal, you may feel like putting your head down on the desk or throwing your free-response packets at the proctor and screaming like a maniac before running out of the room. Don't let this happen to you! Simply close your eyes for a few seconds (but not too long) and take a deep breath before returning to your work. It will all be worth it when you get your AP score!

How to Study for the AP Exam

If you've left yourself plenty of time to study for the AP Exam:

Highlight the areas in this book that you have trouble remembering and review any notes you may have taken in class. It may help if you form a study group with a few of your classmates, since explaining the subject matter ensures you've retained the information. Together with your study group, go through the bold terms listed in the index of this book (these are the key terms most likely to be on the AP exam), and quiz yourself. If you can't remember the concept behind a particular term, go back and review the indicated page. Also, flip through your textbook and take another look at the important diagrams. In the weeks before the AP exam, focus more on the key concepts rather than trying to memorize facts. Take as many practice tests as possible. In doing so, time yourself and simulate the exam environment (that may mean turning off the music). Try to finish studying early so you can relax and mentally prepare in the days before the exam.

If you have less than two weeks before the AP Exam:

DON"T READ THE REVIEW SECTIONS IN ORDER! Go through the Table of Contents and circle the topics you don't remember at all. Read those sections first. Try to read as much as you can, but don't overload. A nervous breakdown can only hurt your score!

The Day of the Exam

Make sure you bring the following:
- Two number-two pencils and an eraser for the multiple-choice section
- A dark-blue or black pen for the free-response section
- A watch (it may NOT have an alarm or a calculator)
- Depending on your proctor, you may be allowed to bring water and a small snack to consume during the short break (in between the multiple-choice and free-response sections)

Don't bring anything that will get you kicked out of the testing room! You may NOT bring books, calculators, or other electronic devices. Don't do anything disruptive or dishonest like ripping a page out of your test booklet or continuing to work after time is up.

Once you've packed up everything you need on test day, relax! Have fun scoring major points on the exam. Good luck!

PART II:

REVIEW OF KEY TOPICS

ENERGY FLOW IN ECOSYSTEMS

Laws of Thermodynamics

The First Law of Thermodynamics states that energy is neither created nor destroyed under normal conditions. It may be transferred, but the total amount of energy remains the same.

The Second Law of Thermodynamics states that with each successive energy transfer, less energy is available to do work because some of it is diffused as heat. Even though the total amount of energy remains the same (First Law of Thermodynamics), the amount of *usable* energy is reduced. Thus, energy must be continuously supplied to Earth to keep ecosystems running. That energy comes from the sun.

Photosynthesis

Photosynthesis is the process by which green plants capture the light energy from the sun and convert it into useful, high-quality chemical energy in the form of organic molecules. It supports nearly all life on earth. Photosynthesis occurs in the leaves of plants, which contain chlorophyll molecules that carry out photosynthetic reactions. Of the light that hits the surface of the Earth, 45% is visible light, and only 1-2% is ultimately available for photosynthesis. The formula for photosynthesis is as follows:

$$\text{solar energy} + 6H_2O + 6CO_2 \longrightarrow 6O_2 + C_6H_{12}O_6$$

In other words photosynthesis requires solar energy, water, and carbon dioxide, and results in oxygen and glucose (sugar). Photosynthesis is important in the carbon cycle, explained later, since all organisms breathe in oxygen and let out carbon dioxide in the process of **cellular respiration**, which reverses photosynthesis by breaking down glucose for energy.

Living Systems

Living systems are organized into species, populations, communities, ecosystems, and the biosphere. A **species** is composed of all organisms that are genetically similar enough to reproduce and create live, fertile offspring. A **population** consists of all members of a species that live in the same area at the same time. As we get wider in scope, a **biological community** is defined as all the populations living and interacting in an area. A community and its physical environment make up an **ecosystem**. It is significant to note that ecosystems are composed of both biotic (living) factors, like trees and animals, and abiotic (nonliving) factors, like water, rocks, and minerals. The **biosphere** is the total of all ecosystems on the planet.

Food Chains and Food Webs

One major property of ecosystems is **productivity**, the amount of **biomass** (biological material) produced in a given area during a given period of time. **Primary productivity** is the productivity of plants through photosynthesis. **Secondary productivity** is the rate of accumulation of herbivore and carnivore biomass.

A **food chain** is a linear chart showing the flow of energy in an ecosystem. An organism's feeding position in an ecosystem is its **trophic level**. The arrows in a food chain connect the trophic levels and always point to where the energy is going. Here are some of the key players in a food chain:

1. **Primary producers** are photosynthesizing organisms (the plants), which support the rest of the food chain.

2. Primary consumers are also called **herbivores** (eat plants); they eat the primary producers. **Consumers** cannot carry out photosynthesis and get their nutrients and energy by eating other things.

3. Secondary consumers eat the primary consumers, tertiary consumers eat the secondary consumers, and so on. They are all called **carnivores** because they eat meat. **Omnivores** eat both plants and meat. **Scavengers**, like vultures, consume animals that are already dead.

4. **Detritivores**, such as worms and ants, consume detritus (litter, debris, and dung).

5. **Decomposers**, such as fungi and bacteria, complete the final breakdown of organic matter and return nutrient to the soil to fertilize the producers.

An example of a terrestrial (land-based) food chain is drawn below. Keep in mind that decomposers and detritivores act on all other trophic levels.

Grass	Beetle	Frog	Hawk
Primary Producer	Primary Consumer	Secondary Consumer	Tertiary Consumer

A **food web** is more complicated because it contains many interconnected food chains and an organism can occupy more than one trophic level (for example, an owl would feed on both mice, which are primary consumers, and snakes, which are secondary consumers).

Ecological Pyramids

Food chains are usually not very long because there is less energy available at each trophic level, since energy is lost as heat at each trophic level and is also used for the individual's metabolism. The general rule to remember (**the ten percent rule**) is that 10% of energy available at one trophic level is transferred to the next trophic level. This means that most ecosystems have a huge number of primary producers

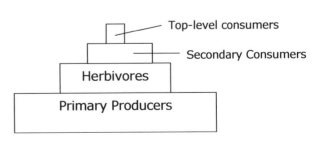

supporting fewer primary consumers, supporting even fewer secondary consumers. Thus, the amount of energy, biological material, and number of individuals at each trophic level can be represented with **Pyramids of Energy**, **Pyramids of Biomass**, and **Pyramids of Numbers**, respectively, with stacked-up rectangles getting smaller as you move up. A generic ecological pyramid is drawn on the previous page.

BIOGEOCHEMICAL CYCLES

Matter is anything that has mass and takes up space. According to the **Law of Conservation of Matter**, matter is neither created nor destroyed but is transformed and recycled over and over again. As a result, elements and compounds essential to life are cycled endlessly through living things and through the environment. On a global scale, this occurs through the **biogeochemical cycles**. In reference to the cycles, a **sink** takes in and stores the element or compound, while a **source** releases it.

Water Cycle

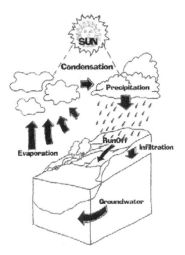

Water exists in three forms: solid (ice), liquid, and gas (water vapor). The water cycle is driven by solar energy, which continuously **evaporates** water from the oceans. Water vapor is also released from plants through **transpiration**. As the water vapor rises and cools, it **condenses** to liquid and falls back down as **precipitation**. Over land, water travels on the surface as **runoff** or **percolates** (seeps through) the soil to join groundwater or **aquifers** (underground freshwater supply). The water eventually evaporates or transpires from plants to restart the cycle. The water cycle (also called the **Hydrologic Cycle**) is therefore driven by solar heat, which causes evaporation.

Carbon Cycle

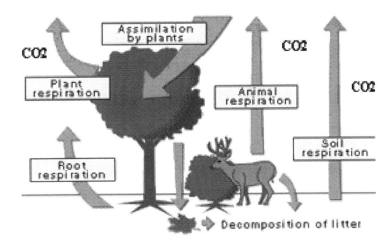

Carbon is the structural component of all **organic** molecules. The carbon cycle is mostly driven by photosynthesis, through which plants incorporate CO_2

into organic molecules, and cellular respiration, which releases CO_2 as a byproduct. However, human activity has drastically increased the amount of CO_2 because combustion of fossil fuels is a carbon source (this leads to more global warming, since carbon dioxide is a greenhouse gas). Carbon sinks include plants, the ocean, and calcium carbonate ($CaCO_2$, the main component of limestone and coral reefs). When animals eat plants, they use the carbon to build their tissues, and when they die, that carbon rejoins the cycle.

Nitrogen Cycle

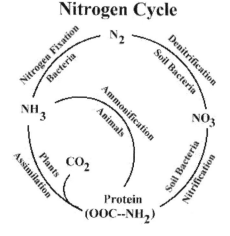

Plants cannot take in atmospheric nitrogen, N_2, but instead acquire nitrogen through the nitrogen cycle. **Nitrogen-fixing bacteria** found in the soil and in the root nodules of legumes (members of the bean family) fix N_2 by converting it to ammonia (NH_3), which can be directly **assimilated** by plants. From there, other bacteria can also convert ammonia to nitrites and nitrates, which can also be used by plants and transferred to animals when those plants are eaten. Lightning also fixes some nitrogen. Nitrogen reenters the environment when decomposers break down wastes and dead organisms. It can also reenter through **denitrification**, the process by which special denitrifying bacteria convert ammonia back into N_2. Humans have significantly altered the nitrogen cycle through the creation of nitrogen-containing chemical fertilizers, which serve as another nitrogen source.

Phosphorus Cycle

The two mineral cycles are those that involve phosphorus and sulfur. Phosphorus has not atmospheric form, so it travels very slowly. The cycle begins when phosphorus compounds **leach** from rocks over time (water percolates through and carries minerals). Plants take in this inorganic phosphorus, assimilate it into organic molecules, and pass it on to consumers. Decomposition returns phosphorus to the cycle. An important phosphorus sink is within sediments deep in the oceans, which return via geologic uplifting of the sea floor. Humans have affected the cycle by creating chemical fertilizers that contain excess phosphorus, which often runs off into lakes and oceans, causing algal blooms

The Phosphorus Cycle

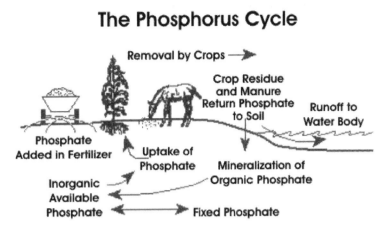

Source: Busman et al., 1997.

and eutrophication (discussed later; excess nitrogen causes the same problem.)

Sulfur Cycle

Most of Earth's sulfur is tied up underground in rocks and minerals. Weathering, volcanic eruptions, and emissions from deep seafloor vents release this inorganic sulfur. Sulfur is also released through biogenic deposits of certain organisms, like phytoplankton. Sulfur cycles through ecosystems when it is taken in by plants and transferred to consumers. This sulfur reenters the cycle when decomposers break down dead organisms (sulfur is a component of some proteins). Furthermore, human activity has released large quantities of atmospheric sulfur through the burning of fossil fuels, which has resulted in a greater incidence of acid precipitation and has increased pH level in many habitats.

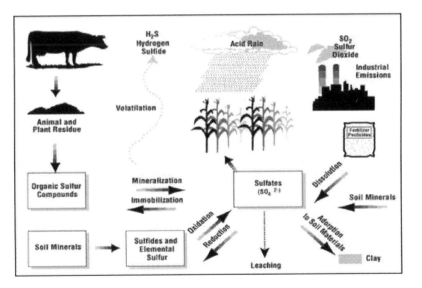

BIODIVERSITY

Biodiversity is the amount of genetic, species, and ecological diversity in an ecosystem.

Theory of Evolution/Natural Selection

Most scientists attribute Earth's biodiversity to **evolution**, generally defined as the changes in the genetic composition of populations over successive generations. According to Charles Darwin, evolution occurs through a process called **natural selection**, better known as "survival of the fittest". Since organisms produce more offspring than can actually survive and because there is genetic variation among offspring, the organisms with the traits best suited to the particular environment will survive and pass on those traits. Natural selection explains the pesticide treadmill faced by farmers and antibiotic resistant bacteria, both of which will be discussed in subsequent sections.

Divergent evolution occurs when new species branch off from a shared ancestral species, as with humans and apes evolving from a shared primate ancestor. In contrast, **convergent evolution** occurs when unrelated species develop similar traits because they develop under similar environmental conditions. For instance, sharks and dolphins both have streamlined bodies, not because they are related, but because they both adapted to marine habitats.

Threats to Biodiversity

Species extinction refers to the elimination of an entire species and is a natural part of biodiversity. However, human activities over the past century, such as the ones listed below, have drastically accelerated the rate of extinction.

1. **Habitat Destruction**: fragments species into small, isolated populations vulnerable to natural catastrophes. Habitat loss through deforestation is the #1 threat to biodiversity!

2. **Hunting and Fishing:** An example is the Passenger Pigeon (extinct due to over-hunting and habitat loss).

3. **Commercial Products**: Smuggling of rare products/live specimens. An example is the African Elephant poached for its ivory tusks.

4. **Introduced/Exotic Species**: Also called "bio-invaders", these organisms lack natural predators in the new environment and quickly use up the resources, killing off the native species. An example is the Kudzu Vine, introduced to the US from Japan, which smothers everything in its path from trees to utility lines.

5. **Genetic Assimilation**: Species disappear because genes are diluted due to crossbreeding with closely related species, as with hatchery-raised salmon.

Legislation Protecting Biodiversity

The Endangered Species Act is a US law identifying endangered, threatened, and vulnerable species and regulating commercial and recreational activities involving them. It requires the US Fish and Wildlife Service to create **Recovery Plans** detailing how listed populations will be revived.

CITES (Convention on International Trade in Endangered Species) is an international agreement regulating trade in living specimens and products derived from listed endangered species. It is difficult to enforce because of smuggling.

SPECIES INTERACTIONS

Predation

Ecologically, a **predator** is defined as any organism that feeds directly upon another living organism, whether or not it kills its prey. Thus, parasites, herbivores, carnivores, and pathogens are all considered predators, but scavengers, detritivores, and decomposers, whose food is already dead, are not. Predators are important in ecosystems because they help maintain stable populations and reduce competition among their prey.

The process in which species exert selective pressure on each other is called **coevolution**, and is common between predator and prey. As the predator becomes more efficient and finding and feeding, the prey becomes better at escape. An example is the relationship between the lynx (predator) and the snowshoe hare (prey).

Competition and Territoriality

Another type of antagonistic relationship within a community is competition. Organisms compete for food, water, shelter, mates, and other limited resources. There are two kinds of competition: **intraspecific competition** occurs between members of the *same* species, whereas **interspecific competition** is when two *different* species compete. To avoid competition, organisms often resort to territoriality of to resource partitioning, which are discussed below.

The term **territoriality** refers to when an animal defends a well-defined space against invaders. Having a territory guarantees its owner access to shelter and food.

Symbiotic Relationships

Symbiosis occurs when members of two or more species live together intimately. The three types of symbiotic relationships are mutualism, commensalism, and parasitism.

1. **Mutualism**: symbiotic relationship in which both members benefit. An example of mutualism is the relationship between coral and algae. The coral harbors algae within its tissues, providing it with shelter, while the algae is photosynthetic and provides the coral with food (carbohydrates).

2. **Commensalism**: symbiotic relationship in which one member benefits, and the other remains unharmed. Epiphytes are plants that grow on the tops of trees. Their relationships with the trees represent commensalism because the epiphytes gain increased light, while the trees do not lose anything.

3. **Parasitism**: symbiotic relationship in which one member benefits, and the other is harmed. As noted earlier, parasitism is also a form of predation. The species that benefits is called the parasite, while the one that is harmed is the host. An example of parasitism is the tapeworm (parasite) that lives within and feeds off of some humans (host), making them sick.

Defense Mechanisms

Evolution has resulted in a wide array of defense mechanisms. These include toxic chemicals (as with poisonous snakes), body armor (as with turtles), spikes and thorns for plants, and camouflage (when organisms blend in with their surroundings). Another type of defense mechanism is mimicry. **Batesian mimicry** occurs when harmless species evolve colors or body shapes that mimic poisonous species. **Mullerian mimicry**, in contrast, is when two species, both of which are poisonous, evolve to look alike. This way, predators can learn to avoid them more quickly.

ADAPTING TO THE ENVIRONMENT

Habitat and Niche

An organism's **habitat** is the place or set of environmental conditions in which it lives. Another term, **ecological niche**, is defined as the role a species plays in a biological community. In describing an organism's niche, one must include how a species obtains food, its interactions with the biotic and abiotic factors of its surroundings, its range of tolerance, and what services it provides the community. More specifically, the **fundamental niche** of a species is the potential niche it can biologically occupy, while its **realized niche** is the role it actually plays. A common analogy to clarify the difference between habitat and niche is that an organism's habitat is it "address", while its niche is its "occupation".

An organism can be categorized as having a generalist niche or a specialist niche. **Generalists** are typically very adaptable and are therefore in less danger of extinction. They tolerate a wide range of environmental conditions, can eat a wide variety of foods, and are able to live in a broad range of habitats. Examples include flies, cockroaches, mice, and rats. In contrast, **specialists** live in very specific types of habitats, can tolerate only a narrow range of environmental conditions, and are very picky with regards to food sources. Examples of organisms with a specialist niche include the giant panda and the orangutan.

The Law of Competitive Exclusion

The more similar the niches of two species, the more they will compete for the same resources. According to the **law of competitive exclusion**, no two species in the same ecosystem can occupy exactly the same ecological niche. To avoid or reduce competition, populations of some species will migrate to another area, undergo resource partitioning, or become extinct. **Resource partitioning** is defined as dividing up scarce resources such as food or shelter space so that many species can survive in a single habitat. This may involve witching to a less readily available food source or hunting for the same food at a different time of the day. An example of the law of competitive exclusion and resource partitioning is the Galapagos Finches studied by Charles Darwin. The different species of finches evolved beaks of different shapes and sizes so that each could rely on a different food source and thereby reduce competition.

Tolerance Limits and Limiting Factors

Every living thing has limits to the environmental conditions it can endure. More than a century ago, Justus von Liebig proposed that the single factor in shortest supply relative to demand, the **limiting factor**, is the critical determinant in species distribution. Another ecologist later expanded on this principle by stating that every environmental factor has both minimum and maximum levels, or **tolerance limits**, beyond which a particular species cannot survive. The *optimal range* is where the species is most abundant, while closer to the tolerance limits is the *region of physiological stress*. Beyond the tolerance limits is the *zone of intolerance*, where the species is absent. Tolerance limits exist for temperature, salinity, moisture level, nutrient supply, and pH. The single factor closest to these tolerance limits is called the **critical limiting factor**.

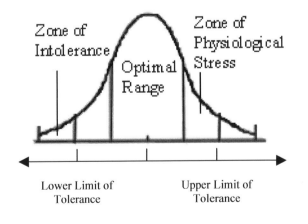

COMMUNITY ECOLOGY

Keystone Species

A **keystone species** is a species whose impact on its community or ecosystem is much more influential than would be expected based on biomass. In other words, it is the species with the most important niche, which, if removed, would cause the ecosystem to fall apart. Keystone species may be top predators who keep prey populations stable, pollinators, or even decomposers that aid in the cycling of nutrients.

Community Properties

As noted earlier, one significant property of communities is their productivity. Other community properties include **abundance**, the total number of organisms in the community, and **diversity**, the number of different species. As a general rule, diversity tends to decrease as we move from the equator toward the poles, so tropical forests are one of the most diverse and productive ecosystems. A community's **complexity** describes the number of species at each tropic level. When you think of complexity, think of a food web; the food web would not be very simple if it had thousands of different species at each trophic level. It would be complex. The term **resilience** refers to a community's ability to recover from disturbance, while **stability** includes a community's *constancy* (how much it fluctuates), *inertia* (its resistance to catastrophes), and *renewal* (its ability to repair damage). How are these terms related? The more complex and diverse a community, the more stable and resilient it is in the face of a disturbance. This is the case because if one species is eliminated, there are many other species at the same trophic level that can take its place.

The boundary between two different communities or ecosystems is called an **ecotone**. When this boundary is sharp, there exists a **closed ecosystem**. When one ecosystem gradually blends into another, each of them is called an **open ecosystem**.

Succession

The sequence of changes through which a community passes over time is called **ecological succession**. **Primary succession** occurs when a community begins to develop on a site previously unoccupied by living organisms, like on a new island or on the land left by a receding glacier. On the other hand, **secondary succession** occurs in a destroyed ecosystem where life existed previously, such as in the area around a volcano after it has erupted.

In primary succession, the new site is first colonized by a few hardy **pioneer species**, usually lichens and mosses, which can withstand harsh conditions and lack of resources. As these organisms die, they help provide debris, organic matter, and soil in which other less hardy organisms can flourish. As succession continues, **seral communities** replace the pioneer species and continue to replace each other. Finally, a **climax community** is reached when the community reaches a stable state that resists further change. It is important to note, however, that certain areas are subject to periodic disruptions and may never reach climax (these are sometimes called *equilibrium communities*). One example is the *fire-climax community*, such as the chaparral, coniferous forests, and grasslands, which are continuously shaped and maintained by fire. Fire helps to return nutrients to the soil, to clear dead plant material, and in the case of the coniferous forest, to melt the sap in cones, thereby releasing the seeds.

TERRESTRIAL BIOMES

Biomes are broad, regional types of ecosystems characterized by distinct climate, soil conditions, and biological communities. Temperature and precipitation are the two most important factors determining the distribution of biomes. We will first discuss the different types of terrestrial biomes, which are those that occur on land.

Deserts

The **Desert** biome is characterized by low moisture levels and infrequent precipitation, along with poor-quality, sandy soil. Temperatures fluctuate widely, with high temperatures during the day and cool temperatures at night. Desert plants, such as cacti, have water-storing leaves and thick epidermal layers to reduce water loss. Many animals, such as kangaroo rats and pocket mice, are nocturnal and have highly concentrated urine to minimize loss or moisture.

Grasslands

Grasslands occur where temperature and precipitation are moderate, with enough rain to support abundant grass yet not enough to support trees. The two types of grasslands are prairies and savannas (mostly in Africa). The soil of the grasslands is considered the richest farmland in the world because it is thick and nutrient-rich. In fact, the greatest threat to grasslands is their conversion into agricultural land. Plants have deep roots and are adapted to survive frequent fires. Animals include migratory grazers like the American bison and African wildebeest.

Tundra

The **Tundra** is a treeless biome found at high altitudes (*arctic tundra*) or mountaintops (*alpine tundra*) characterized by cold winters, a short growing season, and permanently frozen topsoil called **permafrost**. Vegetation includes low-growing perennial plants, mosses, and lichens. Animals, like the caribou and mountain goat, migrate or hibernate during winter. Damage to the tundra heals slowly.

Coniferous Forest

The **coniferous forest** is a biome dominated by cone-bearing trees that occurs in a wide range of temperate (mid-latitude) regions. The northern coniferous forest is called the **boreal forest**. Both the southern pine forest and the boreal forest have sandy, low moisture soil and cool temperatures. The northernmost edge of the boreal forest, where it borders the tundra, is the **taiga**, characterized by harsh, cold temperatures and a layer of peat (partially decomposed organic matter). Plants have evolved thin, needle-like leaves with thick waxy coating to reduce water loss.

Broad-leaved Deciduous Forests

Deciduous forests have trees that lose their leaves during winter, and they occur throughout the world where rainfall is abundant. This biome has a dense canopy that protects an under-story made up of annual spring flowers. Deciduous forests have both a warm and frozen season, and temperatures vary. They include a diversity of species, including some that are endangered like Siberian tigers, bears, and cranes. The main threat to this biome is deforestation.

Chaparral

The **chaparral** occurs in areas with a Mediterranean climate (hot, dry summers, cooler winters, low precipitation), and is characterized by thick growth of thorny, evergreen shrubs and frequent fires. Plants have thick leaves coated in wax to withstand fire. Typical animals include jackrabbits, chipmunks, lizards, and many species of birds.

Tropical Moist Forests

Tropical moist forests, although there are many types, all have ample rainfall and uniform temperatures. They are among the most biologically diverse biomes in the world, estimated to hold more than half of all terrestrial plants and insects on Earth. Most nutrients are contained in the bodies of living organisms, and the soil tends to be thin, acidic, and nutrient-poor, meaning that the biome is slow to recover from disruption. Cool **cloud forests** are found on mountaintops where fog and mist always keeps vegetation moist. **Tropical rainforests** occur near the equator where rainfall is abundant and temperatures are warm year-round. Moist tropical forests are threatened by deforestation due to logging, agriculture, development, and mineral extraction.

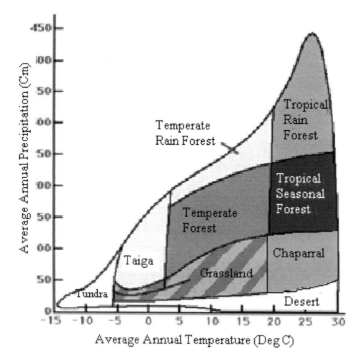

AQUATIC BIOMES

Freshwater

The freshwater biomes you will have to know for the AP exam are lakes, streams, and rivers. Freshwater lakes are characterized by **thermostratification**, or division based on temperature. The **epilimnion** is the warmer water layer on the surface that absorbs sunlight, while the **hypolimnion** is the cooler area closer to the bottom. These warm and cool layers are separated by a thin layer called the **thermocline**, where there is a rapid decrease in temperature over a short distance. The lake bottom is called the **benthos** layer, where there is little oxygen but rich organic matter from the detritus that sinks to the

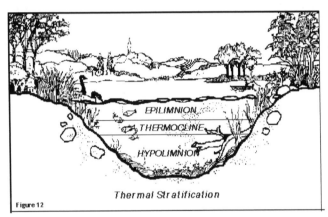

Thermal Stratification

Figure 12

bottom. In autumn and spring, lakes experience **seasonal turnover**, during which waters mix freely to replenish nutrients and oxygen. There is no thermocline during seasonal turnover. Horizontally, the shallow region of a lake closer to shore is called the **littoral zone**, while the deeper region further from shore is called the **limnetic zone**.

Whereas a lake is stagnant, the water in rivers and lakes is constantly moving downstream. The ecosystem around a river is called a **riparian** ecosystem.

Marine

The marine biome (oceans and seas) is characterized by **vertical stratification**, or division into vertical layers. The **photic zone** is closer to the top of the water, and gets enough sunlight to support photosynthesis by algae and phytoplankton.

In contrast, the lower **aphotic zone** does not get enough sunlight for photosynthesis. The **abyssal zone** is the deepest part of the ocean (part of the aphotic zone, since there is no photosynthesis). As in a lake, the ocean bottom is also called the benthos.

Oceans are also divided horizontally. The **intertidal zone** is the area closest to the shore where the tides come in. The open ocean, where there are whales and dolphins, is called the **pelagic zone**.

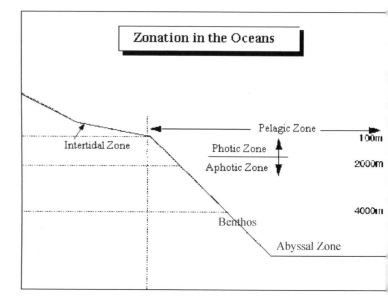

Zonation in the Oceans

Intertidal Zone

Pelagic Zone — 100m

Photic Zone

Aphotic Zone

2000m

Benthos

4000m

Abyssal Zone

Wetlands

A **wetland** is land that remains flooded all or part of the year with fresh or salt water. Wetlands are extremely important because they fulfill several ecological functions. Firstly, wetlands support a high degree of biodiversity (estuaries and coral reefs are two of the most diverse ecosystems on the planet). Moreover, they replenish aquifers and prevent flooding by acting as sponges. Finally, many wetland plants naturally filter sediments and pollutants in the water.

One type of wetland you should remember is an **estuary**, a bay where the river empties into the sea, mixing fresh water with salt water. Estuaries serve as homes for waterfowl and migratory birds and also serve as the grounds where many fish lay their eggs.

RESTORATION ECOLOGY

Restoration ecology involves repairing or reconstructing ecosystems damaged by human activity. This principle is supported by recent court decisions against developers and corporations. **Restoration** is defined as bringing an ecosystem back to its original state before human disruption.

Rehabilitation

Rehabilitation is rebuilding certain elements of an ecosystem without completely restoring to its original condition. This area of restoration ecology is more *utilitarian* in view (the conservation supported by Teddy Roosevelt and Gifford Pinchot), since its aim is to make an ecosystem again usable for humans.

Remediation

When a chemical contaminant is cleaned up from a polluted area, the process is called **remediation**. Often, living organisms are used to clean contaminated areas. The term for this is **bioremediation**. For example, certain wetland plants, such as water hyacinths, can filter out sediment and remove heavy metals and excess nutrients from water. A newer bioremediation technique makes use of **genetically modified organisms** (organisms whose DNA has been manipulated in a laboratory to express a particular trait), specifically bacteria, to destroy harmful chlorinated compounds.

Reclamation and Re-creation

Reclamation is the chemical or physical cleanup and reconstruction of severely degraded areas, such as strip-mining sites. For instance, the **Surface Mining Control and Reclamation Act (SMCRA)** calls for better reclamation techniques after land has been mined, such as filling in open pits (see section on mineral/metal extraction).

OVERVIEW OF POPULATION DYNAMICS

Types of Growth

There are three types of population growth you should be familiar with for the AP exam: exponential, logistic, and irruptive growth. When a population increases by a constant *rate* every year, the population experiences **exponential growth**, represented by a **J-curve**. Exponential growth occurs when there are no limits to growth, meaning resources are endless and environmental conditions are ideal. The maximum slope of the exponential graph gives the **biotic potential** for a population, which is the maximum reproductive rate of a species in ideal circumstances.

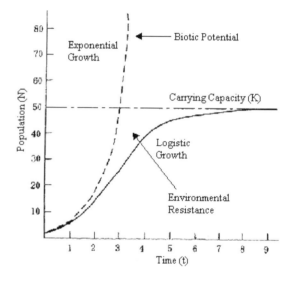

In the real world, however, there are factors such as disease, food supply, and limited space that keep populations in check. Together, these limiting factors make up **environmental resistance** to population growth. Factors limiting population growth can be either **density-dependent** (have a greater impact with larger populations) like predation, competition, or stress, or **density-independent** (have the same effects regardless of population size) like climate. We call the maximum number of organisms that a particular ecosystem can support on a long-term basis the **carrying capacity**. The type of growth that represents reality, taking into account environmental resistance and carrying capacity, is called **logistic growth**, and it is represented by an **S-curve**.

Finally, **irruptive growth**, sometimes referred to as *Malthusian growth*, is a cycle of **population explosions** (rapid increase) followed by **diebacks** (rapid decrease). In this case, the population first **overshoots**, or exceeds, its carrying capacity, and then crashes.

K-selected and *r*-selected Species

Species such as dandelions, rats, and cockroaches that have high reproductive rates and follow an exponential growth pattern are called **r-selected species**. They are typically generalists, have many small offspring at a young age, offer little parental care, and have high mortality for offspring. Their population sizes tend to fluctuate above and below the carrying capacity. On the other hand, **K-selected species**, such as humans and elephants, are usually specialists and follow a logistic growth pattern. They tend to be larger, live longer, produce fewer offspring, and offer more parental care. Moreover, their populations stay fairly stable around the carrying capacity.

Survivorship Curves

Survivorship curves are graphs that represent the number of individuals who survive to a given age. Humans in industrialized countries tend to follow Curve I (see right) because infant mortality

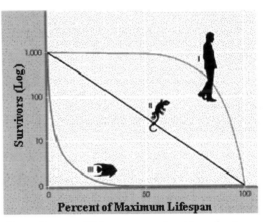

is low. Squirrels, sea gulls, and lizard follow Curve II because death rate is constant. Fish and clams follow Curve III, since infant mortality is high.

Doubling Time

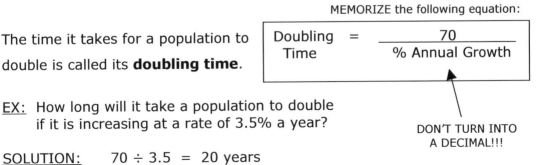

The time it takes for a population to double is called its **doubling time**.

MEMORIZE the following equation:

$$\text{Doubling Time} = \frac{70}{\% \text{ Annual Growth}}$$

DON'T TURN INTO A DECIMAL!!!

EX: How long will it take a population to double if it is increasing at a rate of 3.5% a year?

SOLUTION: 70 ÷ 3.5 = 20 years

HUMAN OVERPOPULATION

The human population is currently over 6 billion.

Important Factors

1. **Natality** (crude birth-rate) is the number of *births* per 1000 individuals.
2. **Mortality** (crude death-rate) is the number of *deaths* per 1000 individuals.
3. **Immigration** is the number of organisms moving *into* an area.
4. **Emigration** is the number of organisms moving *out* of an area.
5. **Fertility** is the number of offspring produced per female in a population.
6. **Fecundity** is the physical ability to reproduce.
7. **Life span** is the maximum number of years a species can survive (about 130 for humans).
8. **Life expectancy** is the average age that an individual is expected to live in a particular time and place (about 76 for women in developed nations).

> Population Growth Rate (%) = birth rate – death rate + immigration rate – emigration rate

EX: A certain country has 14 births and 8 deaths per 1000 individuals. Find the population growth rate assuming there is no immigration or emigration.

SOLUTION: Growth rate = 14/1000 – 8/1000 = 1.4% - 0.8% = 0.6%

Perspectives on Overpopulation

Ecologists argue that human have already reached their carrying capacity and that overpopulation is leading to depletion of resources, environmental destruction, and a decrease in biodiversity. On the opposing side, economists claim that technology is increasing the world's carrying capacity and that a larger population means a larger workforce.

In the late 18th century, **Thomas Malthus** wrote his "Essay on the Principle of Population", in which he predicted that the humans would one day exceed their carrying capacity, and that this would result in war, famine, and disease to reduce the population. People today who agree with Malthus are called **Neo-Malthusians**, and they advocate birth control as a means of stabilizing the population. At around the same time, **Carl Marx** proposed a different view on human population, claiming that exploitation and oppression of the lower classes, not overpopulation, are the causes of pollution, famine, and resource depletion. Today, **Neo-Marxists** believe that the population will only stabilize through **social justice**, a fairer distribution of wealth and resources.

The Developed and Developing Worlds

The developed and developing worlds are divided by an imaginary line, the **Brandt line**. The industrialized, developed world made up of wealthy nations such as the United States and Japan, lies to the north of this line, while poor, underdeveloped countries like India, Bangladesh, and those of Africa and South America lie below the line. A key fact to remember for the AP exam is that the 20% of the population that lives north of the Brandt line uses up nearly 80% of Earth's resources.

Food security, or access to a constant source of food, is a major problem in many underdeveloped countries, especially those in Africa and South/Southeast Asia. This is often connected to **malnourishment**, an imbalance in vitamins and nutrients, or **undernourishment**, not taking in enough calories. Deficiencies in protein, vitamins, or caloric intake can lead to diseases such as *kwashiorkor* or *marasmus*.

Age-Structure Histograms

In an age-structure histogram, each bar represents an age group, with male and female data separated by a vertical line. The histograms that show rapid growth tend to represent developing countries. They have wider bases, since a higher birth-rate means a greater number of young people. In a histogram that shows zero growth, the bars all have the same length because the country has reached **replacement level fertility** (having only enough children to replace the parents

– it is a little more than 2, since some infants die). Spain, Austria, and Greece are experiencing zero population growth. Finally, when the base of the histogram is smaller than the top, it shows negative growth, meaning the population is decreasing. Germany, Sweden, and Bulgaria are experiencing negative growth.

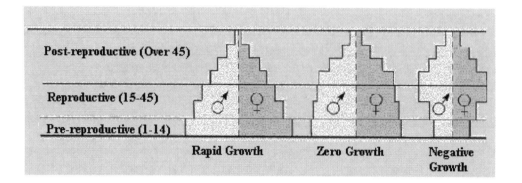

Demographic Transition

When a developing nation gradually improves in living condition and demographic status, the process is called **demographic transition**. The demographic transition model is based on the assumption that once birth and death rates go down, countries become more developed economically. Originally, a developing nation has both a high birth rate and a high death rate. The first step in the transition is to decrease death rate, possibly through medicines or health care programs. At this point, the population grows at an even faster rate, since more individuals are surviving. Gradually, however,

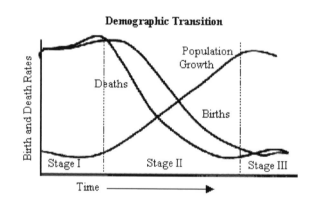

parents have fewer children because they know the infants will survive. As birth rate decreases, the population stabilizes and the nation becomes developed. Most rapidly growing nations of the world, like Kenya and Libya, are in the middle phase of demographic transition, where death rates have fallen, but birth rates remain high.

Urbanization

Urbanization, the growth of cities, is a process that has sped up since the Industrial Revolution. There are several problems associated with cities in the developing world. They often lack infrastructure, organization, and stability, making them sometimes unable to provide adequate food, clean water, housing, jobs, and sanitation for residents. Many third world cities also experience severe air and water pollution. These problems caused many people to move into suburbs or rural areas, resulting in urban sprawl. **Urban sprawl** is the unlimited outward expansion of city boundaries that lowers population density, generates freeway congestion due to increased commuting, consumes open space, and leads to decay in central cities.

HEALTH AND THE ENVIRONMENT

Disease

A **disease** is an abnormal change in the body's condition that impairs physical or psychological functions. Disease-causing organisms, like bacteria, viruses, and parasites, are called **pathogens**. Another important term, **morbidity**, is a measure of the rate of illness. The worldwide burden of disease lies not only in loss of life, but also in loss of productive years, since when people are sick, crops are not planted, meals are not cooked, and children do not learn. **Disability-adjusted life years (DALYs)** are a health measure assessing the total burden of disease on productivity and quality of life.

Recent AP exams have included questions on **emergent diseases**, those not previously known or that have been absent for at least twenty years. Examples include West Nile Disease, caused by a virus transmitted by mosquitoes, and AIDS (Acquired Immunodeficiency Syndrome), caused by the HIV virus. Groups like the World Health Organization (WHO) are fighting certain diseases through *immunizations* (vaccines) and antibiotics. One problem with antibiotics is that bacteria gradually become resistant, since the individuals with the trait for antibiotic-resistance survive and pass on that trait to future generations.

Hazardous and Toxic Chemicals

Chemicals that are dangerous are called **hazardous**, while those that kill cells or alter growth are termed **toxins**. Some chemicals, such as Formaldehyde, are **allergens** (substances that trigger the immune system), and may cause the body to become hypersensitive. One common condition, *"Sick Building Syndrome"*, occurs when office-workers become hypersensitive to chemicals used in building structure. The toxicity of a chemical is measured by its **LD50**, the dose lethal to 50% of a test population; the lower the LD50, the more toxic the chemical. LD50 is usually determined through animal testing.

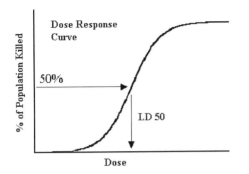

There are four main categories of toxins: neurotoxins, mutagens, carcinogens, and teratogens. **Neurotoxins**, like mercury, lead, and other heavy metals, kill neurons in the nervous system. **Mutagens** cause mutations by altering DNA, while **carcinogens** cause cancer. The **Delaney Clause** to the US Food and Drug Act states that no known carcinogen causing "reasonable harm" may be added to food and drugs. Finally, **teratogens** are toxins such as alcohol that cause abnormal embryonic cell division and result in birth defects.

Toxins are also grouped according to how they react other chemicals or toxins. **Antagonistic toxins** interfere with the effects of other chemicals and work against each other. **Additive toxins** have a cumulative effect, increasing the level of toxicity when many chemicals are mixed together. **Synergistic toxins** cause reactions in which one toxin exacerbates the effect of another, making them both more toxic than they would be alone.

DDT and Biomagnification

Bioaccumulation of a toxin occurs when an organism absorbs and stores the toxin in its tissues. A toxin can enter an ecosystem at a low trophic level, but become more and more concentrated as it moves up the food chain. This is called **biomagnification**, and the best-known example is with the insecticide **DDT**, used extensively in the 1960s but now banned. Due to the widespread spraying of DDT, the chemical entered ecosystems and began biomagnification. By the time it got to predatory birds at the top of the food chain, DDT had reached toxic concentrations, interfering with calcium deposition and causing these birds to lay eggs with thin, brittle shells. As a result, species such as the peregrine falcon and brown pelican became endangered. In her book *Silent Spring*, **Rachel Carson** revealed the harmful ecological effects of DDT and spearheaded the environmental movement.

ECOLOGICAL ECONOMICS

Economic Theory

Based on the ideas of Adam Smith, **classical economics** is the economic theory built on the principle of the free market that forms the foundation of the capitalist system. According to this theory, the economy is governed by the laws of supply and demand. **Supply** is how much of a product is available, while **demand** is the amount of the product that consumers will buy. **Market equilibrium** is the point at which the demand for a good is equal to its supply. Another important term is **marginal cost**, is the cost to produce one more unit of a good.

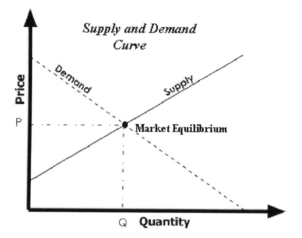

According to classical and neoclassical (more recent) economic theory, when resources run out, one must simply look for a substitute. On the other hand, **ecological economics** asserts that certain resources like biodiversity are irreplaceable. Its goal is to create a **steady-state economy** characterized by recycling of materials, low birth and death rates, and emphasis on efficiency and durability of goods.

Resources

A **resource** is defined as anything capable of creating wealth or giving satisfaction. There are two types of *natural resources*: renewable and nonrenewable. **Renewable resources**, such as organisms (trees), sunlight, and air, are those that are naturally replenished, whereas **nonrenewable resources** like fossil fuels, minerals, and metals, exist in finite amounts. *Intangible* *resources* are another category of resources that includes factors such as open space, beauty, and wisdom, whose value cannot be grasped in terms of price.

In his article **"The Tragedy of the Commons"**, Garret Hardin described that under an **open access system** where everyone has unregulated access to a resource, the resource will be degraded by self-interest. For instance, if many farmers share a single pasture, each will put as many cattle as possible to maximize his own profit, until the land is finally destroyed by overgrazing and trampling. Hardin instead suggested a **communal resource system**, where each person in the community is given a sense of responsibility to take care of the resources, instead of giving everyone unlimited access.

A final point to review is the relationship between resource-use and technology. In a more advanced society, technology brings about efficiency so that fewer resources are wasted. Contrastingly, in a *frontier economy* (underdeveloped), limited access to technology means that resources are used less efficiently.

Measuring Wealth and Quality of Life

Gross National Product (GNP) is a measure of wealth equal to the total of all goods and services produced in a national economy. It is the most commonly used measure of a country's economic growth. The problem with GNP is that it doesn't account for natural resource depletion or ecosystem damage. This is because industries tend to **externalize costs** by disregarding resources for which the producer does not actually pay (such as the value of soil lost to erosion or reduced water quality). Instead of GNP, ecologists prefer to use the **Human Development Index (HDI)** to measure quality of life. It takes into account per capita income, distributional equity, natural resource depletion, environmental damage, and the value of unpaid labor.

Cost-Benefit Analysis

A **cost-benefit analysis (CBA)** is the process of accounting and comparing the costs and benefits of a project before it is enacted. CBA considers who or what is being affected, the potential outcomes, and possible alternatives. This usually helps the environment, since the potential ecological damage is considered for any major federal project.

Organizations and Green Businesses

The *World Trade Organization (WTO)* is an association of more than a hundred nations that meet discuss international trade. The *World Bank* and *International Monetary Fund* are organizations that lend money to needy nations and fund international projects to aid underdeveloped nations. A recent grassroots movement to aid underdeveloped nations involves the wealthiest nations forgiving their debts. *Microlending*, when small banks give loans or equipment to individual families in poor nations, is another helpful development. Finally, the wealthier nations of the world may forgive a poor nation's debt if, in return, that nation sets off a particular area of land as a nature preserve. This is called a *debt-for-nature swap*.

Green businesses are environmentally friendly companies aimed at creating a more sustainable future. They utilize practices such as efficient energy use, recycling of packaging and materials, and the production of more durable goods.

ENVIRONMENTAL POLICY AND LAW

NEPA

Environmental policy refers to the official rules concerning the environment that are implemented by the government. The **National Environmental Policy Act (NEPA)** forms the cornerstone for U.S. environmental regulations and laws. NEPA does three important things: first, it authorizes the *Council on Environmental Quality (CEQ)* to oversee environmental conditions; second, it directs federal agencies to take environmental consequences into account in decision-making; finally, it requires an **Environmental Impact Statement (EIS)** for any major federal project. AN EIS discusses the purpose of the project, any alternatives, and its potential effects on the environment.

Environmental policies, and any other types of policy in the U.S., are put into effect through the **policy cycle**, a continuous process through which problems are identified and acted upon. A generic policy cycle is represented to the right.

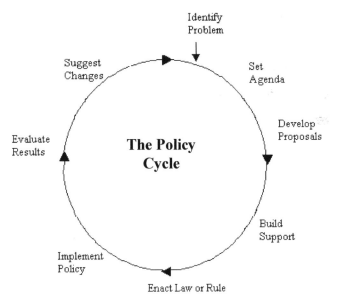

The Precautionary Principle

Wicked problems are those with no simple solution, such as how to save the rainforests or how to deal with global warming. Most environmentalists support the **precautionary principle** in regards to making environmental policy about wicked problems. This principle asserts that we should leave a margin of safety for unexpected developments. In other words, when risks are not fully understood, it is better to be on the safe side.

LAND USE

Soil: Components and Horizons

Soil is a renewable resource made up of a mixture of weathered rock material, partially decomposed organic molecules, and living organisms. The component of soil consisting of decomposed organic matter is called **humus**, which gives soil structure by sticking the particles together. Humus also increases absorption of water and nutrients. There are many different types of soil (classified by the size of their particles), but the best type for farming is *sandy loam*. If soil has a large amount of clay (smallest particles), it is classified as *heavy soil*, whereas if it has more sand and silt, it is classified as *light soil*.

Most soils are stratified into horizontal layers, or **horizons**, which together make up the soil profile. Below is an outline of the various soil horizons.

- **O Horizon**: surface litter.
- **A Horizon**: topsoil; made up of humus, nutrients, and organisms. This is where plants have their roots. Grasslands have a very large A Horizon, which makes them ideal for agriculture.
- **E Horizon**: zone of leaching; where nutrients seep downward.
- **B Horizon**: subsoil; accumulates leached nutrients from the E Horizon.
- **C Horizon**: weathered parent material; partially broken down rock.
- **Bedrock**: solid rock.

Deserts tend to have a very narrow A Horizon and a dense layer of nutrient and salt residue called a **hardpan layer**, beyond which plant roots cannot grow.

Land Degradation

Land is considered degraded when the soil becomes deficient in nutrients, when water does not soak through properly, when there is a lack of vegetation or wildlife, or when water becomes contaminated after mixing with the soil. Several factors contribute to land degradation. These include water and wind erosion, chemical deterioration (such as acidification of soil or soil pollution), and physical deterioration through salinization (too much salt and minerals), compacting, or water logging (saturating) the soil.

Erosion can result in several land problems. Loss of topsoil through erosion results in a decrease in crop production. Erosion also leads to siltation of reservoirs and sedimentation of rivers and lakes (an increase in **turbidity**-muddiness of water), a process that often kills coral reefs. One kind of water erosion, **rill erosion**, occurs when running water cuts small channels into the soil. When rills enlarge, the process is called **gully erosion**. Erosion is particularly severe in areas such as China and Haiti.

The #1 cause of soil degradation is overgrazing of land. Since cattle and pasture animals eat the plants they prefer first, the soil is taken over by less nutritious plants. Eventually, the animals strip the land bare of vegetation and compact the soil with their hooves. This results in **desertification** – degrading of land that was once fertile. Desertification makes land unfit for germinating seeds, since water is no longer absorbed, and it causes a desiccation (drying out) of land and the dying off of larger plants. Some possible ways to avoid overgrazing are to use mixed ruminants, so that all of the animals don't go after the same vegetation, or to harvest native animal species.

Sustainable Agriculture

Sustainable agriculture is an agricultural system that is both economically viable and socially just, yet also ensures ecological sustainability. Some techniques used in sustainable agriculture include soil conservation programs, reduced tillage, and use of cover crops or mulch to prevent erosion. Contour plowing (maintains natural contours of land) and strip farming (using alternate strips of different crops) also reduce the effects of erosion by slowing down the rate of water flow down a hill. Sustainable agriculture also incorporates many of the pesticide-alternatives we will discuss in the next section.

Over the past few decades, food supplies have more than kept pace with the growing human population. This is mostly due to the **green revolution**, a dramatic increase in agricultural production brought about by the development of high-yield, "miracle" varieties of grain. One problem is that green revolution breeds yield more than other strands only when given optimum levels of fertilizer, water, and pesticides.

Forests and Deforestation

The world's forests are classified as either **closed-canopy**, where tree crowns spread out over 20% or more of land area (as in tropical forests) or **open-canopy**, also called *woodland*, where tree crowns cover less than 20% of land area. **Old-growth forests** are the original, ancient forests, like the Redwood Forests in California. Forests play a major role in providing food and shelter wildlife, producing timber and roundwood for human use, anchoring the soil to prevent erosion, and regulating climate through transpiration. Tropical forests make up only 10% of the population, yet contain 50% of species. They are threatened through destructive logging, which leads to less topsoil (due to erosion) and sedimentation of rivers.

More than half of the word's people depend on wood for heating and cooking. These people can reduce their wood consumption by using more efficient metal and ceramic stoves. Sustainable forestry practices, such as replanting mixed species, planting fruit and nut trees, and utilizing legume trees to enrich the soil, are powerful tools against deforestation. Another tool, the *debt-for-nature swap* discussed in the "Ecological Economics" Section, is also helpful in healing deforestation. Finally, techniques of lumber harvesting can be altered. Instead of clear cutting forests (chopping down trees with out discrimination), we can practice selective cutting, which cuts down certain trees on a yearly schedule, and rotates based on area. It is important to note that the US Forest Service currently allows logging to occur in national forests.

Preserves and Wilderness Areas

Nature preserves include recreation areas, historic sites, conservation areas, areas set aside for scientific research, and inviolable preserves, where humans have no access whatsoever. The layout of many nature preserves sets aside **corridors**, connecting habitats to allow species to migrate between protected areas. The **Man and Biosphere (MAB) Program** outlines the ideal layout for a nature preserve: a central core area would be restricted to tourists and only used for scientific research; around the core, a buffer zone would be used for research and tourist facilities; finally, the outermost area of the preserve would be for multiple use, allowing for research and indigenous settlements.

A **wilderness area** is defined as undisturbed land without many roads, where humans may visit but not settle permanently.

The Arctic National Wildlife Refuge (ANWR)

The Arctic National Wildlife Refuge (ANWR) on Alaska's North Slope is the largest wildlife refuge in the US. Petroleum geologists estimate that there could be up to 10 billion barrels of economically recoverable oil beneath the surface. Whereas oil companies advocate opening the refuge to oil exploration and petroleum development, environmentalists assert that this would damage the fragile tundra ecosystem and urge Congress to designate it as a wilderness area.

Since the arctic tundra is an extremely fragile ecosystem, with limited precipitation, a short growing season, and a layer of permafrost, it is particularly susceptible to human impact. Potential impacts on the ecosystem would include disturbing wildlife's natural habitat through the building of gravel roads, contamination of soil and water from oil spills, acid rain and particulate matter emissions from machinery, and deposition of alkaline dust along roads, which would damage vegetation. The animals that would be most adversely affected are the Polar Bear, Musk Oxen, Caribou, and various bird species.

PEST CONTROL

A **biological pest** is any organism that devalues resources useful to humans. **Pesticides** are chemicals used to kill or drive away pests. Some types of pesticides include **herbicides**, which kill plants, and **insecticides** (like DDT), which kill insects. The US is the greatest worldwide consumer of pesticides.

Pesticide Benefits

Benefits to pesticide use include disease control and increased crop production. Firstly, pesticides are helpful because they destroy insects that spread disease. For instance, in Sri Lanka, limited use of DDT kills mosquitoes that spread Malaria. Pesticides also increase crop yield by preventing plant diseases, insect predation, and competition from weeds.

Pesticide Problems

One major problem with pesticides is that they harm non-target species. This was the case when DDT biomagnified and endangered predatory birds in the 1960s. A second problem with overuse of pesticides is pest resurgence, which occurs when pest populations rebound due to pesticide resistance or the killing of their natural predators. The pests with the resistant trait to the pesticide survive and pass on that trait to their offspring, leading to a population of pesticide resistant organisms. This creates a **pesticide treadmill**, a need for constantly increasing doses or new pesticides to prevent pest resurgence. Moreover, pesticides also lead to the creation of new pests, since pesticides end up killing predators that previous kept a number of pests under control. Finally, many pesticides have an adverse effect on human health. Short-term effects could include acute poisoning or illness, while long-term effects include cancer, birth defects, immune problems, or chronic degenerative diseases. For example, Inuit mothers in arctic Greenland who were unintentionally exposed to chemicals like

PBCs (used in pesticides) have breast milk that is considered "toxic waste" and leads to long-term immune and neurological problems in children.

Alternatives to Using Pesticides

A possible alternative to pesticide use is to alter agricultural practices. Planting a cover crop or carrying out crop rotation reduces weeds and insects. Furthermore, switching from a monoculture (single-crop) to a mixed polyculture (many types of crops) field ensures that all of the crops will not be devastated by a single pest. A second alternative to pesticides is reliance on **biological controls**, natural predators, pathogens, or competitors that can regulate pest populations. For example, ladybugs are often used to control aphid populations. Sterile males can also be introduced to reduce mosquito populations. A final alternative to excessive pesticide use is **Integrated Pest Management (IPM)**, a pest control strategy that uses a combination of the techniques listed above and limited use of pesticides as a last resort.

Regulation of Pesticides

You may need to know that that certain US government agencies, namely the EPA, FDA, and USDA, require that all new pesticides be registered. The *Food and Drug Act* also sets tolerance levels for the amount of pesticide residue in food.

EARTH SCIENCE

Plate Tectonics

The Earth's **core**, or innermost center, is a hot mass of metal made up mostly of iron. Surrounding the core is the **mantle**, a liquid layer of hot molten rock called **magma**. The magma in the mantle rises and sinks in circular patterns called **convection currents**. When magma comes up to the surface, it is called **lava**. The outermost layer of the Earth is the cool, lightweight **crust** that floats on the mantle. The most abundant element in the crust is oxygen. The convection currents in the mantle break the overlying crust into a mosaic of huge blocks called **tectonic plates**. As these plates move apart or crash

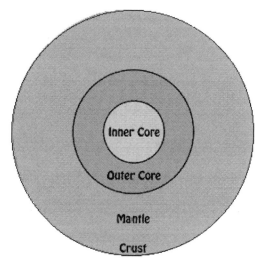

into each other, tectonic activity leads to seafloor spreading, formation of mountains via geologic uplifting, cracks in the crust, volcanoes, and earthquakes. More specifically, when an oceanic plate collides with a continental landmass, the oceanic plate dives under the continent and melts, rising back to the surface as lava. This process, associated with oceanic trenches, is termed **subduction**. It is hypothesized that hundreds of thousands of years ago, the continents were joined in a single landmass now known as **Pangea**.

The Rock Cycle

A **mineral** is a naturally occurring, inorganic (no carbon) solid with a definite chemical composition and an internal crystalline structure. An aggregate of minerals is a **rock**. The web of environmental processes that forms and changes rocks is known as the **rock cycle**.

There are three types of rock: igneous, metamorphic, and sedimentary. **Igneous rocks** are formed when magma cools and solidifies. Quick cooling creates finer-grained rock like basalt, whereas slower cooling produces larger-grained rock like granite. **Sedimentary rocks**, on the other hand, are made up of sediments weathered away from other types of rock and compiled. **Weathering** is a process that occurs when chemical and physical agents gradually break down rock. Examples of sedimentary rocks include conglomerate (compiled pebbles), sandstone (compiled sand), limestone (compiled shells and dead organisms) and shale (compiled mud). Finally, when sedimentary or igneous rocks are transformed under intense heat and pressure, **metamorphic rock** is formed. Examples include marble (pressurized limestone) and slate (pressurized shale).

Extracting Metals and Minerals

The metal with the greatest worldwide consumption is iron. **Strategic metals and minerals** are materials a country cannot produce itself, but that are nevertheless essential for that country (an example is aluminum for the US).

Geologic materials are extracted from the earth as ore (rock that contains needed materials) through placer mining, underground mining, and strip mining. **Placer mining** involves washing pure nuggets from stream sediments using pans or a hose to spray the riverbed. It is environmentally harmful because it chokes stream ecosystems with sediment. **Underground mining**, or tunneling, is extremely dangerous because tunnels can collapse, explode, cause fires, or lead to seeping of contaminated water. **Strip mining** (also called **open-pit mining**) uses trucks to dig huge pits terraced with long ridges called **spoil banks**, which erode easily, are susceptible to leaching, and destroy vegetation by contaminating soil. Groundwater often accumulates in the pit, resulting in a toxic soup that endangers wildlife and nearby watersheds. The **Surface Mining Control and Reclamation Act** calls for better restoration techniques in mining, such as filling in pit mines.

Ore can be processed through smelting and heap-leach extraction. **Smelting** is heating up ore to high temperatures to separate out pure metals. This process gives off sulfur dioxide, which contributes to acid rain. **Heap-leach extraction** uses chemicals to extract pure metals (usually gold) from ore. The ore is piled onto a platform and sprayed with cyanide, which seeps through and dissolves the gold. The dissolved gold collects in water and turns into a solution, which subsequently goes to a plant to be precipitated out. The problem is that cyanide can contaminate groundwater, or mine owners may just walk away from a site without cleaning up.

We can reduce the environmental harm caused by mining by finding substitute materials, like plastic pipes and fiber optic electronics, or by recycling metals. 2/3 of aluminum is currently recycled. This is far more efficient that commercially extracting it from *bauxite* ore. Minimills also re-smelt and reshape iron and steel.

THE ATMOSPHERE AND GLOBAL CLIMATE

Atmospheric Layers

The **atmosphere** is the envelope of gases surrounding the Earth. The most abundant gas in the atmosphere is nitrogen (78%) followed by oxygen (20%). In contrast, Earth's ancient atmosphere was much more massive and was made up mostly of hydrogen and helium. The hydrogen and helium gradually diffused into space, while photosynthesis and volcanic emissions added oxygen and nitrogen, respectively, to create the modern atmosphere.

The atmosphere has four distinct zones of contrasting temperature, due to differences in absorption of solar energy. The **troposphere** is the layer of air closest to the Earth's surface, where convection currents redistribute heat and moisture around the globe and create all weather events. As altitude increases in the troposphere, the temperature decreases. The sharp thermal boundary between the troposphere and the next atmospheric layer is called the **tropopause**. This next layer is the **stratosphere**, where the temperature gets higher because more solar energy is absorbed. The stratosphere is relatively calm and experiences little mixing. For the AP exam, you should remember that the stratosphere contains the **ozone layer** (O_3), which protects life on Earth by absorbing UV radiation.

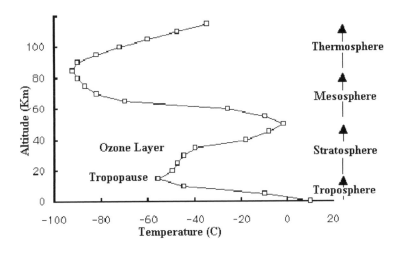

One major environmental problem is the depletion of the ozone layer by **chlorofluorocarbons (CFCs)**, which are currently banned in many nations. Use of CFCs has created a huge hole in the ozone over Antarctica, increasing exposure to UV radiation and resulting in more cases of skin cancer, cataracts, crop failures, and genetic mutations.

Following the stratosphere, the temperature drops again to create the **mesosphere**, or middle layer. The farthest layer from the Earth is the **thermosphere**, consisting of ionized gases heated by solar energy. In the thermosphere, radiation causes ions to glow, forming the **aurora borealis**, or northern lights. No sharp boundary marks the end of the atmosphere.

Climate and Weather

Whereas the term **weather** denotes daily temperature and moisture conditions in a certain area, **climate** refers to long-term weather patterns. Weather patterns are driven by solar energy. For example, uneven heating, with warm air closer to the equator (since the sun shines there directly), produces pressure differences that cause convection currents, wind, rain, and storms. The movement of wind is also related to the rotation of the Earth. This principle is called the **Coriolis Effect**, and on a global scale, it produces reliable wind patterns such as the trade winds and the westerlies. **Jet streams** are forceful winds that circle the Earth at the top of the troposphere.

Much solar energy is used to evaporate water. Globally, water vapor contains a huge amount of stored energy, called **latent heat**, which also affect weather. It is important to note that some of the solar energy hitting the Earth is actually reflected back into space. The reflectivity of a surface is described by its **albedo**.

Other factors that affect weather are **weather fronts**, boundaries between air masses of different temperatures and densities. A **warm front** is a warm air mass that is less dense that surrounding air and leads to wispy clouds, whereas a **cold front** is colder and more dense than the surrounding air and forms big puffy storm clouds. Clashes between warm and cold air lead to cyclonic storms (hurricanes, typhoons, and cyclones) over water, and tornadoes over land. In addition, periodic climatic changes are affected by the orbit of the Earth, the angle of the Earth's tilt, and the wobbling of the Earth's axis. These periodic changes are called **Milankovitch cycles**. A final climatic pattern on the AP exam is **El Nino Southern Oscillation (ENSO)** the alteration every 3-5 years between El Nino, when warm surface water of the Western Pacific (around Indonesia) moves eastward, and La Nina, the intervening years when the warm water remains in the Western Pacific. El Nino leads to wacky weather conditions like excess rain in the Eastern Pacific and droughts or fires in the Western Pacific.

Global Warming and its Effects

Atmospheric gases, like the glass of a greenhouse, transmit sunlight but trap heat inside. This is called the **Greenhouse Effect.** The heat-trapping gases are **greenhouse gases** such as carbon dioxide (CO_2) from respiration and combustion, Methane (CH_4) from coal mines and landfills, Nitrous Oxides, CFCs, and Sulfur Hexafluoride (SF_6), the gas in medical inhalers. Since the Industrial Revolution, human activity has caused an increase in the release of greenhouse gases, and consequently a gradual rise in global temperatures appropriately called **global warming**. Interestingly, **aerosols** (tiny water droplets suspended in the air) are thought to cool temperature by reflecting sunlight, but they are not the answer to global warming because they don't last long in the air.

The rise in global temperature has caused sea ice and alpine glaciers (on mountaintops) to recede, which could increase water levels and destroy habitat. Plants and animals are also affected because the temperatures may surpass their range of tolerance. For instance, as temperatures rise, coral reefs undergo bleaching that kills off their mutualistic algae. Furthermore, global warming could contribute to a change in ocean circulation and the occurrence of severe storms. Warmer temperatures lead to the proliferation of insects and rodents that carry diseases. Lastly, global warming melts the permafrost in the tundra, releasing pockets of methane previously locked in the frozen layer.

The **Kyoto Protocol** is an international agreement to reduce greenhouse gas emissions. US representatives refused to sign because it sets tighter limits for industrialized countries.

AIR POLLUTION

Air Pollutants and The Clean Air Act

Some air pollution comes from natural sources, such as volcanoes or bacterial decomposition, but pollution that results from human activity is described as **anthropogenic. The Clean Air Act of 1970** identified and set limits for the **criteria pollutants** (also called **conventional pollutants**), the seven major air pollutants that are considered the most serious threat to human welfare. The Clean Air Act also set primary standards, intended to protect human health, and secondary standards, to protect property, crops, and visibility. The criteria pollutants are listed below. They are definitely worth memorizing!

1. **Sulfur dioxide (SO_2)**: Natural sources include sea-spray and oceanic vents. Anthropogenic sources include the burning of coal and oil. Sulfur dioxide oxidizes and dissolves in water to form sulfuric acid, which falls to earth as **acid deposition** (acid rain, further described below).

2. **Carbon monoxide (CO)**: CO is a colorless, odorless, highly toxic gas produced by incomplete combustion of fuel. It inhibits respiration in humans by binding to hemoglobin and preventing absorption of oxygen.

3. **Particulate material**: Particulates are particles that float in the air, such as dust, ash, soot, smoke, or pollen. They reduce visibility, and breathing them in can damage lung tissue.

4. **Volatile Organic Compounds (VOCs)**: VOCs are organic gases, such as methane. In nature, they are given off in small quantities by plants. Anthropogenic sources are industrial plants, the burning of hydrocarbons (like benzene in gasoline), and vinyl chloride used in plastic production.

5. **Nitrogen oxides (NO$_x$)**: A natural source of nitrogen oxides is the bacteria in the nitrogen cycle. The main anthropogenic source is combustion of fossil fuels. Nitrogen oxides are a major component of photochemical smog. NO$_x$ may also change into nitric acid, which can be another cause of acid deposition.

6. **Ozone**: Whereas stratospheric ozone is good, protecting us from UV rays, ozone in the troposphere is a harmful photochemical oxidant and a component of smog. **Ambient** (in the surrounding air) ozone has an acrid odor and damages vegetation, animal tissues, and building materials. It is formed when solar energy drives a reaction with nitrogen oxide.

7. **Lead**: Lead accounts for a majority of metallic air pollution (other polluting metals are mercury from burning coal, nickel, uranium, and plutonium). Lead previously came from leaded gasoline, but may also be released through mining or manufacturing. Lead and mercury are both neurotoxins that damage the nervous system and cause brain damage or retardation.

Primary pollutants are those released directly in hazardous form, whereas **secondary pollutants** are released in nontoxic form, then react to become toxic. Examples of a secondary pollutant are photochemical smog (nitrogen oxides or ozone) and atmospheric acids (sulfur oxides).

Besides the criteria pollutants, the Clean Air Act of 1970 also identified **unconventional pollutants**, which are not as common as criteria pollutants, but are especially toxic. Examples include asbestos and PCBs.

Indoor air pollutants can also be extremely dangerous. In developed countries, the most important air contaminant by far is cigarette smoke. In less developed countries, on the other hand, smoky, poorly ventilated cooking and heating fires represent the greatest source of indoor air pollution. In nations like the US, a major source of radon contamination in houses is the underlying bedrock, which has been connected to lung cancer. A final important form of pollution is aesthetic degradation, in the form of noise or odors.

Since 1970, the Clean Air Act has been updated, and amended. Modifications include reductions of smog, ozone, sulfur oxides, and nitrogen oxides emissions, phasing out CFCs, and tougher standards on fugitive emissions. Furthermore, the EPA has created a new policy of marketing pollution rights, allowing factories to buy and sell pollution permits from each other.

Controlling Air Pollution

Fugitive emissions are those that do not go through a smokestack, such as dust from mining or leaks from industrial valves. Fugitive emissions are difficult to monitor or control. However, the air pollution released by smokestacks *can* be controlled through a variety of methods. Particulate removal can be accomplished using filters or electrostatic precipitators. **Filters** are giant porous bags that fit over a smokestack and trap ashes and soot, allowing air to pass through. **Electrostatic precipitators** are electrically charged devices. Particulates from the smokestack carry opposite charges and stick to the device like a magnet.

Besides particulates, sulfur oxides, nitrogen oxides, and hydrocarbons must also be removed before passing through smokestacks. One way to solve the sulfur oxide problem is to use low sulfur fuel. Alternatively, **fluidized bed combustion** forces high-pressure air through coal and crushed limestone on a combustion bed. The limestone reacts with the sulfur, converting it to a harmless form. A final method to remove sulfur is **flue-gas scrubbing**, which involves treating combustion exhaust gases by spraying them with limestone. This can be done either with liquid limestone (wet scrubbing) or dry limestone (dry scrubbing).

To remove nitrogen oxides, factories can modify the flow of air during combustion. Cars utilize a **catalytic converter** to convert nitrogen oxides into other chemicals. To remove hydrocarbons (VOCs), cars use the *PCV*, which recycles unused fuel and returns it to the engine.

Impact of Air Pollution

Some health conditions associated with air pollution are **bronchitis**, an inflammation of the bronchial tubes that makes it hard to breathe, and **emphysema**, or lung disease, which destroys the alveoli. Moreover, air pollution has a negative impact on plants by oxidizing chlorophyll, thereby reducing photosynthesis in a condition called **chlorosis**. Pollutants in the air also cause mottling, or discoloring of the leaves.

One particular type of air pollution, acid deposition (rain has lower pH), damages fish eggs, plants, and small invertebrates in and around lakes because the pH is past their tolerance limits. Furthermore, acid deposition causes nutrients to leach out of soil. The acid also reacts with aluminum in soil and makes it precipitate out. It kills *mycorrhizae*, a symbiotic root fungus that helps trees absorb water. Finally, acid deposition causes problems for humans by damaging buildings and sculptures. Acid can be neutralized by crushed limestone and marble, since these substances contain calcium carbonate, a base.

WATER USE

Sources of Water

The total amount of water taken from a source is **withdrawal**, whereas **consumption** is the fraction of withdrawn water that is evaporated, absorbed, or lost in transmission as a result of human use. Globally, agriculture claims about 70% of total water withdrawal, much of which is lost to evaporation. **Drip irrigation** is a water-efficient technique that delivers small quantities of water directly to the plants.

Most of the world's water supply is held in oceans, and the amount of time a water molecule spends there (3000 years) is called its **residence time**. Ocean water is *not* part of the **renewable water supply**, the freshwater available to humans. In fact, freshwater makes up only 2.5% of global water. Sources of freshwater include groundwater (biggest source), glaciers, rivers, streams, lakes, ponds, wetlands, and the atmosphere. Groundwater is sometimes found in **aquifers**, underground rivers trapped between geologic layers.

The atmosphere holds the smallest percentage of water and has the fastest turnover rate. An important term related to water in the atmosphere is **humidity**, which describes the amount of water vapor in the air. The temperature at which condensation occurs is the **dew point**. Sometimes, particulates floating in the air help condensation occur by providing a surface onto which water vapor can gather. These particulates serve as **condensation nuclei**. The principle of condensation nuclei forms the basis of *cloud seeding*, where particulates are sprayed into the air to encourage rain. Mountains can also affect rain patterns. Usually, the up-slope side of a mountain is wet and rainy, while the down-slope **rain shadow** is dry and experiences less rain.

The Water Table

In discussing groundwater, there are a number of relevant terms you should know for the AP exam. Rain that doesn't evaporate or runoff percolates through the soil in a process called **infiltration**. The upper layers of soil, containing both water and pockets of air, make up the **zone of aeration**. As you move downward, the lower soil layers are completely waterlogged, making up the **zone of saturation**, which is the source of most wells. The top of the zone of saturation is called the **water table**.

Depleted Groundwater

The section of the water table where groundwater is being depleted faster than it is renewed is called the **cone of depression**. An example is the Ogallala Aquifer in the Great Plains. Depletion of groundwater can lead to a number of problems. Excess water withdrawal may cause an aquifer to

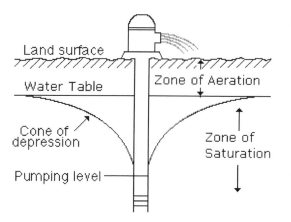

collapse, resulting in **subsidence**, or sinking of land. Eventually, the ground may open up and form a sinkhole. Another negative consequence of groundwater depletion is **saltwater intrusion**, when saltwater contaminates an aquifer, since it moves in to fill the void left by depleted freshwater.

When groundwater in an area is being used up faster than it can be renewed, the area experiences **water stress**. To increase water supply to dry areas, the residents can try **cloud seeding**, mentioned earlier, which involves spraying particulates into the air to act as condensation nuclei, inducing rain. Another technique to increase water supply is **desalinization**, which involves removing salt from ocean water. This method takes up a lot of money and energy, and requires the construction of special facilities. A less reasonable technique that has been attempted is to tow an iceberg to a dry region as a source of fresh water. They may also transfer water from somewhere else, or build a dam to block river flow.

Environmental Impact of Dams

Dams are extremely beneficial in providing water and hydroelectricity, but these benefits are environmentally and socially costly. Large dams often raise the water level, flooding towns and farmlands and displacing people from their homes. For example, China's Three Gorges Dam, the largest dam in the world, submerged several cities and forced villagers to relocate. Another social problem associated with large dams is loss of historic artifacts and economic losses from property damage when cities are submerged. Ecologically, a serious dam problem is the loss of free-flowing rivers, which decreases river flow on the other side of the dam and disrupts the migration of fish populations. This was an issue with the Hetch Hetchy Dam near Yosemite National Park. Furthermore, large dams bring about ecosystem losses, since they collect silt and increase turbidity upstream, while starving streambeds and sandbars downstream. Finally, dams waste tremendous amounts of water from evaporation and through seepage into porous rock beds. For example, Lake Mead and Lake Powell lose huge quantities of water to evaporation each year.

WATER POLLUTION

Point and Nonpoint Sources

Factories, power plants, and oil wells are considered **point sources** because they release pollution directly from specific locations, such as pipes. In contrast, **nonpoint sources**, like runoff from farm fields, logging sites, and urban areas, are harder to monitor or regulate because they have no specific location where they discharge into a body of water.

Categories of Water Pollution

The first major category of water pollution involves infectious agents, which cause diseases such as typhoid, cholera, and hepatitis. The main source of these pathogens is untreated human or animal wastes. Water is usually tested for **coliform bacteria** (such as *E. Coli*) to determine if infectious agents are present, since these bacteria are also present in feces. Included in this category are Red Tides, which occur when dinoflagellates or algae release toxins into the water that damage human health.

The second category of water pollution is oxygen-demanding waste. The amount of dissolved oxygen (DO) is a waterway is a good indicator of water quality. Oxygen is added to water through photosynthesis or diffusion from air, and is removed by respiration. Adding organic material like sewage to water stimulates oxygen consumption by decomposers. Consequently, **biochemical oxygen demand (BOD)**, or the amount of DO consumed by microorganisms, is a standard measure of water contamination. Downstream from a pollution source, microorganisms with a high BOD begin decomposing the pollution, creating a decline in DO termed **oxygen sag**. Upstream from the pollution source is the *Clean Zone*, where normal DO levels support clean-water organisms. Immediately below the source of pollution, DO levels begin to fall as decomposers metabolize waste materials, creating a *Decomposition Zone* where trash fish survive. Farther downstream, in the *Septic Zone*, the water becomes so oxygen depleted that fish die off and only worms and microorganisms survive. Past the Septic Zone, less pollution means fewer decomposers and higher DO, forming a *Recovery Zone*. Past the Recovery Zone is another Clean Zone.

Water pollution can also be caused by plant nutrients like nitrates and phosphates from fertilizers, animal waste, or detergents. When these nutrients enter a waterway, it causes algal blooms that reduce water clarity and diminish oxygen levels in a process called **cultural eutrophication**. The resulting lack of oxygen creates a **Hypoxic Zone** (also called a **Dead Zone**), where fish have died. Contrastingly, when there are low levels of nutrients in a water body, it is considered **oligotrophic**.

An additional category of water pollution is made up of inorganic pollutants, including metals, non-metallic salts, acids, and bases. Metals such as mercury, lead, and tin can undergo biomagnification in aquatic ecosystems.

Besides the categories already mentioned, water pollution may include sediment, mostly from agricultural erosion. The sediment fills up reservoirs, suffocates coral reefs, and ruins spawning grounds. In oceans, oil spills and dumping of plastics that can entangle animals are major sources of pollution. A last category is **thermal pollution**, which occurs when power plants release heated water into rivers, which disrupts aquatic organisms and decreases oxygen levels.

The Clean Water Act

The goal of the **Clean Water Act** is to make all surface waters fit for fishing and swimming. The Act makes it unlawful for anyone to discharge any pollutant from a point source into navigable waters unless he first obtains a permit identifying the name and quantity of the pollutant. The Clean Water Act requires that the "Best Practicable Technology" (BPT) be used to clean up point sources, while the "Best Available Technology" (BAT) be used to clean up toxins. It also funds the construction of sewage treatment plants, includes provisions for protecting wetlands, and requires that state governments identify polluted waterways within their boundaries. Furthermore, the Clean Water Act assigns a maximum daily pollution amount allowed for each pollutant and body of water in the US, called the **Total Maximum Daily Load**. The Act has been modified over the years to switch the focus from sewage and point sources to the entire watershed. Modifications have also given states increased responsibility in enforcing the Act.

Wastewater Treatment

There are a number of steps in municipal sewage treatment. **Primary treatment** filters out solid material and takes out sediments with a grit chamber. During this step, settling tanks allow some dissolved organic solids to fall out as **sludge** The next step, **secondary treatment**, removes

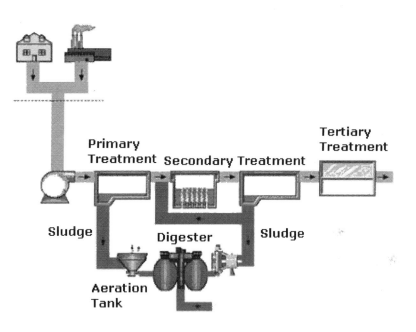

disease-causing pathogens by adding chlorine. This step also involves treating sludge using either lagoons or aeration tanks. The **lagoon system** places sludge in shallow basins for several months, allowing for the natural, gradual degradation of sewage. In contrast, an **aeration tank** pumps air through a tank filled with aerobic bacteria that break down the sludge more quickly. The aeration tank process for treating sludge is also called the **activated sludge process**. Sludge may also be sent to digesters, in which bacteria further decompose it and release methane (natural gas) as a byproduct. The last step in wastewater treatment is **tertiary treatment**, which gets rid of dissolved nutrients such as nitrates and phosphates. This is often accomplished by allowing effluent to flow through a wetland. **Effluent** is a term that refers to water being released or treated.

Some American cities and many developing countries rely on a **septic tank** instead of municipal sewage treatment. Septic tanks, which must be cleaned and emptied periodically, hold solid waste to be decomposed by bacteria. The septic tank system allows liquids to percolate through drain fields, where they are aerated to presumably kill germs. Underdeveloped countries that cannot afford septic tanks instead rely on outdoor pit toilets called outhouses or use human waste as "night soil" to fertilize rice paddies. These methods often spread pathogens into the food supply.

SOLID WASTE

Disposal Methods

The **waste stream** is the steady flow of varied wastes we all produce, from domestic and yard garbage to industrial, commercial, and construction refuge. There exist many ways to dispose of waste. In most developing countries, the predominant method of waste disposal is unregulated open dumping. For example, Manila, in the Philippines, has an open dump called "Smoky Mountain", which contributes to constant smoldering fires, poor sanitation, foul odors, vermin, groundwater contamination, and disease. The second method is ocean dumping, a practice that often entangles marine animals. Ocean dumping is now prohibited by federal legislation. In 1990, an international agreement made at the **London Dumping Convention** (a.k.a. **"The Law of the Sea"**) ended all ocean dumping of plastics, oil effluent, and industrial waste by signatory countries.

The most common method of waste disposal in American and European countries is placement in regulated **sanitary landfills**, where solid wastes are compacted and buried under soil. To control hazardous substances that may seep through dirt, all US landfills are required to have the following structure: an impermeable clay and/or plastic lining underlies and encloses the storage are, while drainage systems around the liner monitor leaking chemicals. The problem is that suitable places for landfills are becoming harder to find due to rising land prices. Many people refuse to have landfills or incinerators in their areas, since such vicinities are considered **Locally Unwanted Land Uses (LULUs)**. These people join under the slogan **Not In My Backyard (NIMBY)**.

Although most industrialized nations have agreed to stop shipping hazardous and toxic waste to less-developed countries, this continues to be used as a major method of waste control. In the US, Indian reservations are exempt from some state and federal regulations, and have become a target for the exporting of solid wastes. In another case, thousands of tons of toxic incinerator waste from Taiwan were unloaded from a ship in the middle of the night and dumped into a Cambodian village, causing nerve damage and respiratory illness in residents.

Another waste disposal method commonly used in the US is burning, or **incineration**. The heat from incineration can produce steam used directly for heating buildings or generating electricity. The remaining ash also takes up far less landfill space. In some plants, garbage is sorted as it comes in to remove unburnable or recyclable materials, resulting in **refuse-derived fuel** that has a higher energy content. Other plants simply dump everything that fits into a giant furnace, utilizing an approach called **mass burn**. However, incineration is very expensive. Furthermore, resulting residual ash often contains toxic components.

Reducing Waste

One way to reduce waste is to reuse materials, thereby reducing the waste stream. Another possibility is **recycling**, which in terms of waste management refers to the reprocessing of discarded materials into new products. Recycling saves money, energy, raw materials, and land space, while also reducing pollution and encouraging individual awareness. Cons are that recycled products are not as popular and that recycling often requires an initial investment and construction of special facilities. Potential incentives for recycling could include setting prices of natural resources at their real cost (instead of reducing prices to stimulate industry) or requiring government agencies to purchase a minimum amount of recycled material. **Demanufacturing** is the disassembly and recycling of obsolete consumer products like television sets, computers, phones, and washing machines.

Instead of burying organic material in landfills, yard waste and agricultural residue can be turned into useful products through **composting**: the breakdown of organic matter under aerobic (oxygen-rich) conditions. Compost makes a nutrient-rich soil amendment that improves crop yields, slows erosion, and aids in water retention. methane generation. Organic wastes can also be decomposed in large, oxygen-free digesters to produce methane, a valuable energy source.

Hazardous and Toxic Wastes

Hazardous waste is defined by the government as any discarded material containing substances known to be (1) fatal to humans or lab animals in low doses; (2) carcinogenic, toxic, mutagenic, or teratogenic; (3) easily ignitable, explosive, highly reactive, or corrosive. Hazardous waste is either recycled, converted to less hazardous form, bioremediated, or placed in permanent retrievable storage or in a secure landfill. Since hazardous waste sites are associated with questions of liability, many cities have large areas of polluted properties called **brownfields** that have been abandoned because of real or suspected contamination.

Two important federal laws regulate hazardous waste management and disposal in the US. The **Resource Conservation and Recovery Act (RCRA)** requires shippers, generators, and disposers to keep meticulous account of every hazardous waste they handle and what happens to it from generation to ultimate disposal... or from "cradle to grave".

The Comprehensive Environmental Response, Compensation, and Liability Act (CERCLA), better known as the **Superfund Act** (just remember CERCLA and Superfund, you don't have to know what it stands for!) is aimed at rapid containment, cleanup, or remediation of abandoned toxic waste sites. It authorizes the EPA to undertake emergency actions to clean up these sites using the **superfund**, a revolving financial pool created for that purpose. Superfund money comes from taxes on producers of toxic and hazardous wastes. Recently, however, the funds have dwindled because Congress let the tax expire. The sites considered especially hazardous to human health and environmental quality are categorized as **National Priorities List (NPL) Sites**, to undergo immediate cleanup under the Superfund Act. Since the superfund in drying up, many NPL site shave not been contained.

SOURCES OF ENERGY

Work is the application of force through distance, while **energy** is the capacity to do work. Some common energy units are Joules (J), Calories (cal), and BTUs. A *joule* is the amount of work done when a force of 1 Newton is exerted over 1 meter. A *calorie* is the amount of energy to heat 1 g of water 1°C. The unit that you're most likely to see on the free response section is the **BTU**, the energy to heat 1 lb of water 1°F.

Commercial Energy Consumption Worldwide

Nuclear 6%
Hydro 7%
Wind, etc 2%
Oil 40%
Gas 22%
Coal 23%

Nonrenewable: Coal, Oil, and Natural Gas

Oil, coal, and natural gas are types of **fossil feuls**, energy-rich chemicals derived from wastes and dead organisms buried for millions of years.

Geologists expect that within a decade, oil production will peak and begin to decline, making other energy sources more attractive. The largest supply of proven oil reserves are in Saudi Arabia (25%). Altogether, Middle Eastern countries control 2/3 of world oil and they have joined with other oil-rich nations to form the **Organization of Petroleum Exporting Countries (OPEC)** to exert international political influence. Oil drilling and shipping contribute to soil and water pollution, as demonstrated by oil spills like that of *Exxon Valdez* (See section on ANWR). Some unconventional oil resources include **shale oil**, which consists of kerogen trapped in sedimentary rock, and **tar sands**, made up of oil and sand coated with hydrocarbons. However, these oil sources are often difficult and expensive to extract and refine.

World coal deposits are vast, and at present rates of consumption, proven reserves are estimated to last another 200 years. China has the largest coal reserves in the world, while Russia and North America also hold great amounts. Coal comes in a variety of forms. **Lignite**, the softest, has low sulfur content, but does not provide much energy. **Bituminous** coal has higher sulfur content and is more efficient. The hardest and most desirable coal is **anthracite**, which has the highest energy yield and has low sulfur content. Mining for coal releases toxins like mercury and is associated with collapsing tunnels and fires, erosion, leaching of chemicals, sedimentation, contamination of groundwater, and destruction of habitat, along with respiratory diseases like "black lung". Mining also contributes to acid rain due to sulfur dioxide emissions and global warming due to carbon dioxide released from combustion.

Natural gas is cleaner burning than oil or coal, and can reduce global warming, since it produces only half as much CO_2 as coal. However, natural gas is difficult to transport or store because it requires an expensive pipeline network. Some unconventional sources of natural gas include methane hydrate, which is trapped in the tundra's permafrost, and methane digesters, which trap methane released when decomposers break down human and animal waste.

Nuclear Power

Radioactive **isotopes** are unstable substances with a different number of neutrons than their corresponding elements. The **half-life** of a radioactive isotope is the time it takes for half of a sample to decay. For example, if the half-life of a substance is 10 years and you have 100 g, after 10 years there will be 50 g left. After 20 years, there will be 25 g left. The most commonly used fuel in nuclear power plants is **U-235**, a naturally occurring isotope of uranium that must be purified from ore, which normally contains only .7% uranium. The U-235 is then concentrated into cylindrical pellets, and stacked into hollow metal rods. About 100 of these rods bundled together make a **fuel assembly**. Thousands of fuel assemblies are placed in a steel vessel to form the **reactor core**. Nuclear power is based on the principle of **nuclear fission**, which involves splitting the nucleus of a isotope to release energy and neutrons. When U-235 is packed tightly in a reactor core, the neutrons released by one atom will trigger the fission of another uranium atom, creating a **self-sustaining chain reaction** that releases vast amounts of energy. The chain reaction is moderated in a power plant by a neutron- and heat- absorbing cooling solution between the fuel rods, and water surrounding the reactor core to absorb excess heat. In addition, **control rods** of neutron-absorbing chemicals like boron or graphite are inserted into spaces between fuel assemblies to shut down the reaction, or are withdrawn to allow it to proceed. If the control rods or cooling solution stop working, the result is an **amplifying chain reaction**, in which the fission reaction grows and grows until a nuclear explosion occurs.

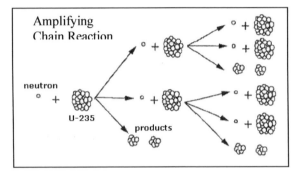

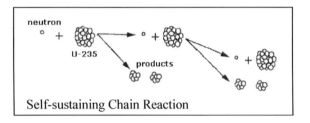

A majority of the world's nuclear plants are **Pressurized-Water Reactors (PWR)**, designed so that water circulates through the core to absorb heat. The water is then pumped to a steam generator, where it heats a secondary water-cooling loop. Steam from the secondary loop drives a turbine-generator to produce electricity. A diagram of a PWR nuclear power plant is included on Pg. 75. In Europe and the former USSR, a common reactor design is the **Boiling Water Reactor** that uses graphite both as a moderator and as the structural material for control rods. This design is not as safe because graphite can melt. The main problem besides safety issues associated with nuclear power is the disposal of radioactive waste produced during mining, fuel production, and reactor operation.

Alternative Energy

Since nonrenewable sources of energy are limited in supply, alternative sources are necessary to provide sustainable energy. The simplest use of solar energy is

passive heat absorption, using natural materials or absorptive structure with no moving parts to simply gather and hold heat. An example is a greenhouse on the south side of a building, or a heat-absorbing Trombe wall made of glass bricks. In contrast, **active solar systems** pump a heat-absorbing fluid through a collector. In the case of high-temperature solar energy, parabolic mirrors are used to focus sunlight on the water pipe. Solar energy can be stored in insulated water bins or in *eutectic chemicals*, which absorb tremendous amounts of heat. **Photovoltaic cells** capture solar energy and directly covert it to an electric current. These devices produce no pollution, have negligible maintenance costs, are durable, and provide renewable energy.

An alternative energy source common in developing nations is biomass, which includes organic materials like wood, charcoal, agricultural or timber waste, and dung. Using biomass as fuel emits less SO_2 and reduces bioinvader species. However, it is extremely time-consuming, releases particulate matter (soot) and carbon oxides, and leads to deforestation. One biomass alternative is **biodiesel**, which directly uses vegetable oil instead of gas in diesel engines.

Hydroelectric energy is a renewable energy source that generates electricity when water flows through a turbine, usually in a dam. As mentioned earlier, large dams lead to many problems (Pg. 62). **Tidal energy** is related to hydroelectric energy uses tides along the coast to generate electricity. However, it could contribute to coastal erosion or destroy habitats. Another energy source that depends on the ocean is **Ocean Thermal Electric Conversion (OTEC)**, which uses temperature differences between warmer surface water and cooler deep water to generate electricity with a heat exchanger and turbine.

The ultimate source of wind energy is the sun, which drives the movement of air masses. Most wind turbines have two to three propeller blades. A **wind farm** is a concentration of wind generators producing commercial electricity. Some advantages of wind energy are that it is abundant, renewable, nonpolluting, and causes minimal environmental disruption. However, it requires expensive storage during peak production times to offset non-windy periods. In addition, wind farms are aesthetically unpleasant and kill birds when they get caught in the turbines.

Another alternative energy source is **geothermal energy**, which uses heat from the Earth, as in hot springs, to generate electricity. The Earth's heat boils water held underground and converts it to steam, which can be harnessed by a turbine. Additional wastewater is often added underground to generate more steam. Some problems with geothermal energy are that many geothermal sites are seismically active, pipes are noisy, and water that is returned to the ground to increase steam yield may be contaminated.

A final alternative energy source is a **fuel cell**, a device that uses ongoing electrochemical reactions powered by hydrogen to produce an electrical current. Fuel cells are very similar to batteries, except that, instead of recharging them with an electrical current, you add more fuel for the chemical reaction. All fuel cells consist of a positive electrode (**cathode**) and a negative electrode (**anode**) separated by an **electrolyte solution** (or proton exchange membrane), a material that allows the passage of charged ions, but is impermeable to electrons. [Note: you can remember that the anode is negative because you can't write the letter A without " - "]. In a fuel cell, hydrogen is passed over the anode, while oxygen is passed over the cathode. Electrons are removed from hydrogen atoms at the anode to produce hydrogen ions (protons, H^+) that migrate through the electrolyte medium to the cathode.

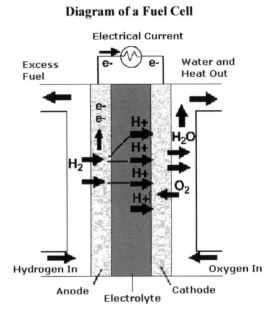

There, they reunite with the original electrons that have traveled through an external circuit and oxygen atoms to make water (H_2O). While the electrons are flowing through the circuit connecting the electrodes, they are creating an electrical current. To operate a fuel cell, a **reformer** is also necessary to strip hydrogen from fuels such as natural gas, ammonia, or vegetable oil. A fuel cell run on pure hydrogen and oxygen produces no waste products except water and heat, but coupled with a reformer, it releases low levels of carbon dioxide.

Conserving Energy

One way to conserve energy, described above, is to rely more on renewable sources of energy. We can also increase the fuel efficiency of automobiles, or utilize electric or hybrid vehicles (hybrids have dual engines that alternate between gasoline and electricity). To increase energy efficiency in the home, it is important to have proper insulation, such as curtains, weather-stripping for heat escape, and double-paned windows. Instead of relying on a thermostat, blankets can be used indoors. Homeowners may also utilize passive solar heat by having larger windows that let in more sunlight. In industry, energy can be conserved through heat recovery (reuse heat given off by generators), more efficient motors, and recycling of steel and other materials. Heat recovery could include **cogeneration**, which reuses waste heat for other purposes like heating water.

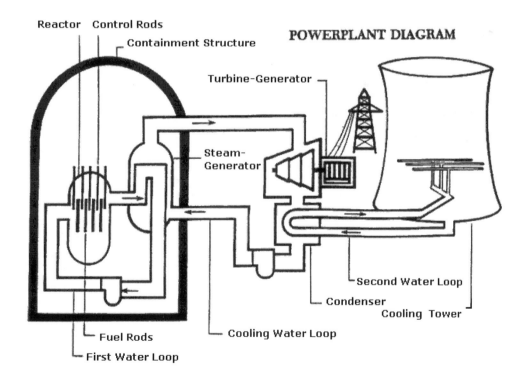

ENVIRONMENTAL DISASTERS

You will probably run into a couple of questions about these environmental disasters on the multiple-choice section of the AP exam. Knowing the basic information stated here will easily score you a few extra points. Note: don't memorize the dates! They are only included to give you a basic time frame!

Chernobyl, Ukraine

In 1986, Chernobyl, Ukraine (then part of the USSR) was the site of the worst nuclear accident in the history of nuclear power. The plant's operators were careless and violated procedures, causing the graphite-moderated Boiling Water Reactor to lose its coolant water and explode. The subsequent blasts and fires released radioactive matter into the atmosphere. Two people were initially killed by the explosion, while thousands later suffered of radiation illnesses or cancers.

Love Canal, New York

Early in the 1940s, a chemical company purchased the abandoned Love Canal to use as a dump, filled it to capacity with toxic waste, and covered the toxins with dirt. The company then sold the land to the area's Board of Education. The site was then used as an elementary school and playground. Heavy rains in 1977 caused the toxins to seep into the soil, making people in the neighborhood suffer serious illnesses such as Epilepsy, liver malfunctions, miscarriages, skin sores, rectal bleeding, and birth defects. The resulting public outcry encouraged Congress to pass CERCLA (Superfund) in 1980.

Bhopal, India

The Bhopal disaster of 1984 was the worst industrial disaster in history. It was caused by the accidental release of huge quantities of toxic MIC gas from a pesticide plant. The MIC leak killed thousands outright and injured an estimated 200,000 others, leaving them with neurological, vision, and respiratory ailments.

Three Mile Island, Pennsylvania

In 1979, the nuclear power plant at Three Mile Island suffered a partial core meltdown. The cooling system had failed, building up pressure in the reactor core. Although no identifiable injuries immediately occurred, the disaster caused a serious decline in the popularity of nuclear power in the US.

Minamata, Japan

From 1932 to 1968, a Japanese petrochemical and power company dumped an estimated 27 tons of mercury compounds into Minamata Bay. Thousands of townspeople whose regular diet consisted of fish from the bay developed mercury poisoning, a neurological syndrome that would later be called "Minamata Disease". The Minamata incident led to over 900 deaths and to the physical suffering of thousands of people.

IMPORTANT INDIVIDUALS

Rachel Carson

Author of <u>Silent Spring</u> and founder of the modern environmental movement, who revealed the harmful ecological effects of the pesticide DDT. See Pg. 38.

Theodore Roosevelt and Gifford Pinchot

US President Roosevelt moved forest management into the Department of Agriculture, naming Pinchot the first chief of the new Forest Service. Roosevelt and Pinchot established the framework of the national forest, park, and wildlife refuge system and helped pass game protection legislation. Their policies were based on *utilitarian conservation*; the principle that forests should be saved not for nature's sake, but to provide jobs and homes for people.

John Muir

Influential conservationist who worked to preserve wildlife from commercial exploitation. His efforts helped to establish Yosemite National Park in California. He also founded the Sierra Club, and served as its first president.

Aldo Leopold

Often considered the father of wildlife ecology, Aldo Leopold was the author of the <u>Sand County Almanac</u>, in which he outlined his "land ethic". He advocated restoration of damaged land combined with stewardship of nature.

Garrett Hardin

Author of "The Tragedy of the Commons", an essay about the degradation of resources under the open access system. See Pg. 40.

ENVIRONMENTAL LAWS AND AGREEMENTS

International Laws

1. **Kyoto Protocol**: Agreement to reduce greenhouse gas emissions. Pg. 54.
2. **Agenda 21**: UN program to make development environmentally and socially sustainable in the 21st century- **sustainable development**. Adopted at the Rio Earth Summit in Brazil.
3. **Montreal Protocol**: Agreement to phase out the use of substances that deplete the ozone layer, including CFCs, halons, and carbon tetrafluoride.
4. **CITES**: Convention on International Trade in Endangered Species. Pg. 19.
5. **The London Dumping Convention:** "The Law of the Sea". Pg. 67.

National Laws

1. **Endangered Species Act**: Pg. 19.
2. **Wilderness Act**: Established a national wilderness preservation system and officially defined wilderness.
3. **NEPA**: National Environmental Policy Act. Pg. 42.
4. **CERCLA (Superfund) and SARA**: Pg. 69.
5. **Surface Mining Control and Reclamation Act**: Pg. 50.
6. **Resource Conservation and Recovery Act (RCRA)**: From "cradle to grave." Pg. 69.
7. **Clean Air Act**: Pg. 55-56.
8. **Clean Water Act**: Pg. 64-65
9. **Delaney Clause to the US Food and Drug Act**: Pg. 38.

INDEX OF KEY TERMS

Don't worry... you don't have to memorize all of the terms listed below to do well on the AP exam! However, the ones *most likely* to be found on the exam are in bold. Go through the bold terms in the index and quiz yourself. If you can't remember the concept behind a certain term, review the indicated page. Although the other terms still may be tested, you'll be in good shape if you know all the ones in bold.

A
Abundance, 24
Abyssal zone, 30
Acid deposition, 56
Activated sludge process, 65
Active solar systems, 72
Additive toxins, 39
Aeration tank, 65
Aerosols, 55
Agenda 21, 79
Albedo, 54
Allergens, 38
Ambient, 57
Amplifying chain reaction, 72
Anode, 74
Antagonistic toxins, 39
Anthracite, 71
Anthropogenic, 56
Aphotic zone, 30
Aquifers, 15, 60
Arctic National Wildlife Refuge (ANWR), 47
Arora borealis, 54
Assimilation, 16
Atmosphere, 53

B
Batesian mimicry, 21
Benthos, 29
Bioaccumulation, 39

Biochemical oxygen demand, 63
Biodiesel, 73
Biodiversity, 18
Biogeochemical cycles, 15
Biological community, 12
Biological controls, 49
Biological pest, 48
Biomagnification, 39
Biomass, 12
Biomes, 26
Bioremediation, 31
Biosphere, 12
Biotic potential, 32
Bituminous, 71
Boiling Water Reactor, 72
Boreal forest, 27
Brandt line, 35
Bronchitis, 59
Brownfields, 69
BTU, 70

C
Carcinogens, 39
Carl Marx, 35
Carnivores, 13
Carrying capacity, 32
Catalytic converter, 58

Cathode, 74
Cellular Respiration, 11
Chaparral, 27
Chlorosis, 59
Chlourolfuorocarbons, 53
CITES, 19
Classical economics, 40
Clean Water Act, 64
Climate, 54
Climax community, 25
Closed ecosystem, 24
Closed-canopy, 46
Cloud forest, 28
Coevolution, 20
Cogeneration, 75
Cold front , 54
Coliform bacteria, 63
Commensalism, 21
Communal resource system, 41
Complexity, 24
Composting, 68
Comprehensive Environmental Response, Compensation, and Liability Act (CERCLA), 69
Condensation nuclei, 60

Condensation, 15
Cone of depression, 61
Coniferous forest, 27
Consumers, 12
Consumption, 60
Control rods, 72
Convection currents, 50
Conventional pollutants, 56
Convergent evolution, 18
Core, 50
Coriolis Effect, 54
Corridors, 47
Cost-benefit analysis (CBA), 41
Criteria pollutants, 56
Critical limiting factor, 23
Crust, 50
Cultural Eutrophication, 64

D
DDT, 39
Dead Zone, 64
Deciduous forest, 27
Decomposers, 13
Delaney Clause, 39
Demand, 40
Demanufacturing, 68
Demographic transition, 36
Denitrification, 16
Density-dependent, 32
Density-independent, 32
Desalinization, 61
Desert, 26
Desertification, 45
Detritivores, 13
Dew point, 60
Diebacks, 32

Disability-adjusted life years (DALYs), 38
Disease, 38
Divergent evolution, 18
Diversity, 24
Doubling time, 33
Drip irrigation, 60

E
Ecological economics, 40
Ecological niche, 22
Ecological succession, 25
Ecosystem, 12
Ecotone, 24
Effluent, 66
El Nino Southern Oscillation (ENSO), 55
Electrolyte solution, 74
Electrostatic precipitators, 58
Emergent diseases, 38
Emigration, 34
Emphysema, 59
Endangered Species Act, 19
Energy, 70
Environmental Impact Statement (EIS), 43
Environmental policy, 43
Environmental resistance, 32
Epilimnion, 29
Estuary, 30
Evaporation, 15
Evolution, 18
Exponential growth, 32
Externalize costs, 41

F
Fecundity, 34
Fertility, 34
Filters, 58

First Law of Thermodynamics, 11
Flue-gas scrubbing, 58
Fluidized bed combustion, 58
Food chain, 12
Food security, 35
Food web, 13
Fossil fuels, 70
Fuel assembly, 71
Fuel cell, 74
Fugitive emissions, 58
Fundamental niche, 22

G
Generalists, 22
Genetic assimilation, 19
Genetically Modified Organisms, 31
Geothermal energy, 73
Global warming, 55
Grasslands, 26
Green business, 42
Green Revolution, 46
Greenhouse Effect, 55
Greenhouse gases, 55
Gross National Product (GNP), 41
Gully erosion, 45

H
Habitat, 22
Half-life, 71
Hardpan layer, 44
Hazardous waste, 69
Hazardous, 38
Heap-leach extraction, 52
Herbicides, 48
Herbivores, 12
Horizons, 44

Human Development Index (HDI), 41
Humidity, 60
Humus, 44
Hydroelectric energy, 73
Hydrologic Cycle, 15
Hypolimnion, 29
Hypoxic Zone, 64

I
Igneous rocks, 51
Immigration, 34
Incineration, 68
Infiltration, 61
Insecticides, 48
Integrated Pest Management (IPM), 49
Interspecific competition, 20
Intertidal zone, 30
Intraspecific competition, 20
Introduced species, 19
Irruptive growth, 32
Isotopes, 71

J
J-curve, 32
Jet streams, 54

K
Keystone species, 24
K-selected species, 33
Kyoto Protocol, 55

L
Lagoon system, 65
Latent heat, 54
Lava, 50
Law of competitive exclusion, 22
Law of Conservation of Matter, 15
LD50, 38
Leach, 16

Life expectancy, 34
Life span, 34
Lignite, 71
Limiting factor, 23
Limnetic zone, 29
Littoral zone, 29
Locally Unwanted Land Uses (LULUs), 67
Logistic growth, 32
London Dumping Convention, 67
M
Magma, 50
Malnourishment, 35
Man and Biosphere (MAB) Program, 47
Mantle, 50
Marginal cost, 40
Market equilibrium, 40
Mass burn, 68
Mesosphere, 54
Metamorphic rocks, 51
Milankovitch Cycles, 55
Mineral, 50
Montreal Protocol, 79
Morbidity, 38
Mortality, 34
Mullerian mimicry, 21
Mutagens, 39
Mutualism, 21

N
Natality, 34
National Environmental Policy ACT (NEPA), 43
National Priority List (NPL) Sites, 69
Natural selection, 18
Neo-Malthusians, 35
Neo-Marxists, 35
Neurotoxins, 39
Nitrogen-fixing bacteria, 16

Nonpoint sources, 63
Nonrenewable resource, 40
Not In My Backyard (NIMBY), 67
Nuclear fission, 71

O
Ocean Thermal Electric Conversion (OTEC), 73
Old-growth forests, 46
Oligotrophic, 64
Omnivores, 13
Open access system, 41
Open ecosystem, 24
Open-canopy, 46
Open-pit mining, 51
Organic, 15
Organization of Petroleum Exporting Countries (OPEC), 70
Overshoots, 33
Oxygen sag, 63
Ozone layer, 53

P
Pangea, 50
Parasitism, 21
Particulate material, 56
Passive heat absorption, 72
Pathogens, 38
Pelagic zone, 30
Percolation, 15
Permafrost, 27
Pesticide treadmill, 48
Photic zone, 29
Photosynthesis, 11
Photovoltaic cells, 73
Pioneer species, 25
Placer mining, 51
Point sources, 63
Policy cycle, 43

Population explosions, 32
Population, 12
Precautionary Principle, 43
Precipitation, 15
Predator, 20
Pressurized Water-Reactors (PWR), 72
Primary pollutants, 57
Primary producers, 12
Primary productivity, 12
Primary succession, 25
Primary treatment, 65
Productivity, 12
Pyramids of biomass, 14
Pyramids of energy, 14
Pyramids of numbers, 14

R
Rachel Carson, 39
Rain shadow, 60
Reactor core, 71
Realized niche, 22
Reclamation, 31
Recycling, 68
Reformer, 74
Refuse-derived fuel, 68
Rehabilitation, 31
Remediation, 31
Renewable resource, 40
Renewable water supply, 60
Replacement level fertility, 35
Residence time, 60
Resilience, 24
Resource Conservation and Recovery Act (RCRA), 69

Resource partitioning, 22
Resource, 40
Restoration ecology, 31
Restoration, 31
Rill erosion, 45
Riparian, 29
Rock cycle, 50
Rock, 50
r-selected species, 33
Runoff, 15

S
Saltwater intrusion, 61
Sanitary landfills, 67
Scavengers, 13
S-curve, 32
Seasonal turnover, 29
Second Law of Thermodynamics, 11
Secondary pollutants, 57
Secondary productivity, 12
Secondary succession, 25
Secondary treatment, 65
Sedimentary rocks, 51
Self-sustaining chain reaction, 71
Septic tank, 66
Seral communities, 25
Shale oil, 70
Sink, 15
Sludge, 65
Smelting, 52
Social justice, 35
Soil, 44
Source, 15
Specialists, 22
Species extinction, 18
Species, 12

Spoil banks, 51
Stability, 24
Steady-state economy, 40
Strategic metals and minerals, 51
Stratosphere, 53
Strip mining, 51
Subduction, 50
Subsidence, 61
Superfund, 69
Supply, 40
Surface Mining Control and Reclamation Act (SMCRA), 31
Surface Mining Control and Reclamation Act, 51
Survivorship curves, 33
Sustainable agriculture, 45
Sustainable development, 79
Symbiosis, 21
Synergistic toxins, 39

T
Taiga, 27
Tar sands, 70
Tectonic plates, 50
Ten percent rule, 13
Teratogens, 39
Territoriality, 20
Tertiary treatment, 65
The Clean Air Act of 1970, 56
Thermal pollution, 64
Thermocline, 29
Thermosphere, 54
Thermostratification, 29
Thomas Malthus, 34
Tidal energy, 73
Tolerance limits, 23
Total Maximum Daily Load, 65

Toxins, 38
"The Tragedy of the Commons", 41
Transpiration, 15
Trophic level, 12
Tropical moist forest, 28
Tropical rainforest, 28
Tropopause, 53
Troposphere, 53
Turbidity, 45

U
U-235, 71
Unconventional pollutants, 57
Underground mining, 51
Undernourishment, 35
Urban sprawl, 37
Urbanization, 37

V
Vertical stratification, 29
Volatile Organic Compounds (VOCs), 56

W
Warm front, 54
Waste stream, 67
Water stress, 61
Water table, 61
Weather fronts, 54

Weather, 54
Weathering, 51
Wetland, 30
Wicked problems, 43
Wilderness Act, 79
Wilderness area, 47
Wind farm, 73
Withdrawal, 60
Work, 70

Z
Zone of aeration, 61
Zone of saturation, 61

PART III:

PRACTICE TEST

ENVIRONMENTAL SCIENCE
Section I
100 Questions
Time – 1 hour and 30 minutes
No Calculators!

Directions: Each set of lettered choices below refers to the numbered questions or statements immediately following it. Select the one lettered choice that best answers each question or best fits each statement. A choice may be used once, more than once, or not at all in each set. On the actual AP exam, you will be bubbling in answers on a separate sheet.

Questions 1-4 refer to the following steps or processes in wastewater treatment.

(A) Activated sludge process
(B) Primary treatment
(C) Secondary treatment
(D) Tertiary treatment
(E) Lagoon system

1. Step that removes nutrients such as nitrates and phosphates from effluent

2. Process that allows for the gradual, natural degradation of sewage by placing sludge in shallow basins for several months

3. Step during which chlorine is added to effluent to kill of disease-causing pathogens

4. Step in which solid material and sediment are filtered out of wastewater

Questions 5-9 refer to the following air pollutants.

(A) Ozone
(B) Sulfur dioxide
(C) Carbon monoxide
(D) Lead
(E) Volatile Organic Compounds (VOCs)

5. Inhibits respiration by binding to hemoglobin and preventing absorption of oxygen

6. Considered beneficial in the stratosphere but harmful in the troposphere

7. Is the pollutant that flue-gas scrubbing is designed to eliminate from power plant smokestack emissions

8. Linked to neurological damage in humans

9. Cause of acid deposition

Directions: Each of the questions or incomplete statements below is followed by five suggested answers or completions. Select the one that is best in each case and then fill in the corresponding oval on the answer sheet.

10. The risks of disposing of toxic chemicals underground were revealed at which of the following locations?

(A) Three Mile Island, Pennsylvania
(B) Bhopal, India
(C) Minamata, Japan
(D) Chernobyl, Ukraine
(E) Love Canal, New York

11. The Kyoto Protocol is an international agreement aimed at addressing which of the following environmental problems?

(A) Ocean dumping
(B) Trade in endangered species
(C) Global warming
(D) Deforestation
(E) Water pollution

12. A country currently has a population of 50 million and a growth rate of 7%. If the growth rate remains constant, what will the population of this country be in 20 years?

(A) 80 million
(B) 100 million
(C) 150 million
(D) 200 million
(E) 400 million

13. Most municipal solid waste is disposed in the US through which of the following methods?

(A) Sanitary landfills
(B) Incineration
(C) Composting
(D) Recycling
(E) Ocean dumping

14. What relationship is exemplified by tapeworms feeding off a human and making the human sick?

(A) Commensalism
(B) Parasitism
(C) Mutualism
(D) Intraspecific competition
(E) Interspecific competition

15. What factor(s) is/are *most* significant in determining the distribution of biomes?

(A) Soil characteristics
(B) Temperature

(C) Precipitation
(D) Geographic location
(E) Both B and C

16. Worldwide, what is the factor creating the greatest threat of species extinction?

(A) Hunting and fishing
(B) Habitat loss
(C) Smuggling of endangered species
(D) Genetic assimilation
(E) Weakening of environmental legislation

17. A population of wild Canadian Geese contains 1000 individuals. How long will it take the population to double if it grows at a constant rate of 3.5% a year?

(A) 70 years
(B) 50 years
(C) 30 years
(D) 20 years
(E) 10 years

18. What is the most abundant gas in Earth's atmosphere?

(A) Oxygen
(B) Carbon dioxide
(C) Hydrogen
(D) Water vapor
(E) Nitrogen

19. Place the following terms in order from narrowest to broadest category:

I. Biosphere
II. Ecosystem
III. Species
IV. Population

(A) I, II, III, IV
(B) III, IV, II, I
(C) III, II, IV, I
(D) I, III, II, IV
(E) IV, III, II, I

20. Photosynthesis is the major source of which of the following gases in Earth's atmosphere?

(A) O_2
(B) CO_2
(C) H_2O (water vapor)
(D) N_2
(E) H_2

21. What treaty or piece of environmental legislation limits international trade in live specimens or products derived from endangered species?

(A) CERCLA

(B) The Montreal Protocol
(C) The Kyoto Protocol
(D) The CITES Treaty
(E) The Endangered Species Act

22. Which of the following is NOT a step in the demographic transition model?

(A) Decrease in death rate
(B) Increase in birth rate
(C) Population stabilizes
(D) Decrease in birth rate
(E) Country becomes developed

23. What was Garrett Hardin's assertion in the "Tragedy of the Commons"?

(A) Under an open access system, resources are likely to be degraded by self-interest
(B) People in a community should not feel responsibility towards their land
(C) Technology will increase the world's carrying capacity
(D) Individuals should be given unregulated access to shared resources
(E) Social justice is the only solution to environmental dilemmas

24. Which of the following embodies the concept of natural selection?

I. The pesticide treadmill
II. Antibiotic-resistant bacteria
III. Polar bears having fur that camouflages with the snow
IV. The different species of finches on the Galapagos Islands

(A) III only
(B) III and IV only
(C) II, III, and IV only
(D) II and IV only
(E) I, II, III, and IV

25. What biome is characterized by low levels of precipitation, a short growing season, and a permafrost layer?

(A) Desert
(B) Tundra
(C) Coniferous Forest
(D) Both A and B
(E) Both B and C

26. Cultural eutrophication can directly lead to which of the following?
I. A Hypoxic Zone
II. Algal blooms
III. Increase in water clarity and oxygen level
IV. Reduction in water clarity and oxygen level

(A) II only
(B) I and II only
(C) I, II, and IV only
(D) I, II, and III only
(E) II and III only

27. Soil bacteria play the most important role in what biogeochemical cycle?

(A) Nitrogen cycle
(B) Hydrologic cycle
(C) Phosphorous cycle
(D) Sulfur cycle
(E) Both A and B

Questions 28-30 refer to the figure below

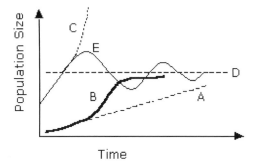

28. Represents the carrying capacity of the population in this particular ecosystem

29. Represents this species' biotic potential

30. Population curve that represents the logistic growth model

31. Worldwide, which of the following sources provides the greatest percentage of commercial energy?

(A) Oil
(B) Nuclear power
(C) Natural gas
(D) Solar energy
(E) Hydroelectric energy

32. Herbivores make up what trophic level?

(A) Primary producers
(B) Tertiary consumers
(C) Quaternary consumers
(D) Primary consumers
(E) Secondary consumers

33. Most of the world's volcanoes are associated with which of the following?

(A) Faulting
(B) Depletion of groundwater
(C) Eutrophication
(D) Mid-continental hot spots
(E) Plate boundaries

34. Which of the following is the best example of a nonpoint source of water pollution?

(A) Thermal pollution from a power plant
(B) Sewer outfall
(C) Contaminated water from an abandoned mine
(D) Factory effluent
(E) Agricultural runoff

35. What are the two major mechanisms in the Carbon Cycle?

(A) Decomposition and erosion
(B) Respiration and photosynthesis
(C) Sedimentation and weathering
(D) Assimilation and deposition
(E) Photosynthesis and transpiration

36. Which of the following is NOT a problem associated with the construction and use of large dams?

(A) Loss of free-flowing rivers
(B) Increased water loss through evaporation
(C) Desertification
(D) Displacing of people from their homes
(E) Disruption of fish migrations

37. What happens to Biochemical Oxygen Demand (BOD) and Dissolved Oxygen (DO) levels immediately downstream from a discharge of organic pollutants?

(A) BOD increases and DO decreases
(B) BOD decreases and DO increases
(C) Both BOD and DO increase
(D) Both BOD and DO decrease
(E) BOD and DO remain the same

38. Which of the following is NOT a typical characteristic of a K-selected species?

(A) Populations remain fairly stable around carrying capacity
(B) Usually larger than r-selected species
(C) Offer high degree of parental care
(D) Tend to be generalists
(E) Have fewer offspring

39. What are the three types of rock in the rock cycle?

(A) Igneous, Metamorphic, and Volcanic
(B) Volcanic, Igneous, and Sedimentary
(C) Granite, Basalt, and Conglomerate
(D) Metamorphic, Sedimentary, and Weathered
(E) Igneous, Metamorphic, and Sedimentary

40. In a soil profile, the C horizon consists of:

(A) The zone of leaching
(B) Surface litter
(C) Topsoil
(D) Weathered parent material
(E) Subsoil

41. Why did the pesticide DDT reduce populations of predatory birds, placing many on the endangered species list?

(A) DDT made predatory birds unable to capture prey
(B) DDT biomagnified and became concentrated in predatory birds, making their egg-shells thin and brittle
(C) DDT biomagnified and became concentrated in predatory birds, interfering with their immune systems and making them sick
(D) DDT is extremely acidic, and killed off predatory birds by disrupting their body's pH
(E) DDT is extremely basic, and killed off predatory birds by disrupting their body's pH

42. Which of the following are problems associated with groundwater depletion?

I. Saltwater intrusion
II. Algal blooms
III. Acidification of aquifers
IV. Subsidence

(A) I only
(B) IV only
(C) I and IV only
(D) I, II, and IV
(E) I, III, and IV

43. Erosion does NOT result in:

(A) Siltation of reservoirs
(B) Sedimentation of rivers and lakes
(C) Increase in crop production
(D) Loss of topsoil
(E) Increase in turbidity of rivers and lakes

44. Researchers have discovered that a certain chemical used in the production of soft vinyl baby toys, when administered in large quantities, presents a potential health hazard. They have not yet determined what dose is harmful. If the decision-makers follow the Precautionary Principle, what will they do?

(A) First assess potential risk by conducting further research, then, if necessary, recall all products containing the chemical
(B) Continue research, then place a warning label on the products only if there is significant risk involved
(C) Halt research until a compromise is negotiated with the baby toy industry
(D) Take no action until an exact harmful dosage is established
(E) Immediately recall from shelves all products containing the chemical until further research is completed and the chemical proven safe

45. Which of the following is an example of a biological control used as an alternative to pesticides?

(A) Introducing ladybugs to reduce aphid populations
(B) Releasing sterile females into a pest population
(C) Crop rotation
(D) Removing all crop residue
(E) Preventing the growth of a cover crop

46. What is the main purpose of control rods in a Pressurized Water Reactor (PWR)?

(A) To reduce radioactive waste produced during fission
(B) To moderate the reactions by absorbing neutrons
(C) To reduce thermal pollution
(D) To produce steam for running the turbine
(E) To act as a heat exchanger between warm and cool water

47. What does it mean if huge quantities of Coliform Bacteria are present in a lake?

(A) The lake has high levels of dissolved oxygen
(B) The lake has a low rate of secondary productivity
(C) The lake has a high rate of primary productivity
(D) The lake is likely to contain infectious agents from untreated waste
(E) The lake will soon transform into a wetland

48. What is the greatest worldwide cause of soil degradation?

(A) Agricultural erosion of topsoil
(B) Overgrazing of land
(C) Acidification of soil
(D) Soil contamination from industrial and urban runoff
(E) Salinization of soil

49. Which of the following is an example of primary succession?

(A) Succession after Mt. Saint Helen's erupted
(B) Succession in an area disrupted by logging
(C) Succession on the land left by a receding glacier
(D) Succession over a filled-in pit mine
(E) Succession in a region destroyed by fire

50. What are some environmental problems associated with strip mining?

(A) Spoil banks erode easily
(B) Soil becomes contaminated, destroying vegetation
(C) A toxic soup of groundwater often accumulates in the pit
(D) Both B and C
(E) All of the above

51. Which of the following is NOT an ecological function performed by wetlands?

(A) Reducing populations of exotic species
(B) Harboring much biodiversity
(C) Replenishing aquifers
(D) Naturally filtering pollutants and sediment
(E) Preventing floods by absorbing runoff

52. The goal to make development socially and environmentally sustainable in the 21st century is referred to as _____and was outlined in the international agreement known as _____

(A) Sustainable progress, NEPA
(B) Sustainable progress, The Montreal Protocol
(C) Progressive development, The London Dumping Convention
(D) Sustainable development, The Montreal Protocol
(E) Sustainable development, Agenda 21

96

53. Which of the following is an example of an emergent disease?

(A) Alzheimer's
(B) Epilepsy
(C) West Nile Virus
(D) Smallpox
(E) Typhoid

54. Negative consequences of urban sprawl include:

(A) Freeway congestion due to increased commuting
(B) Decay in central cities
(C) Consumption of open space
(D) Both A and C
(E) A, B, and C

55. According to the First Law of Thermodynamics,

(A) Matter is neither created nor destroyed, but only transferred
(B) Energy is neither created nor destroyed, but only transferred
(C) Energy may be created, destroyed, or transferred
(D) Matter may be created, destroyed, or transferred
(E) With each successive energy transfer, some energy is dissipated as heat

56. Approximately what percent of the energy available at one trophic level is transferred to the next trophic level?

(A) 10%
(B) 25%
(C) 50%
(D) 75%
(E) 100%

57. In determining the toxicity of a chemical, what is its LD50?

(A) The animal species used to test the chemical
(B) The percentage of the test population that dies from 50 mg of the chemical
(C) The number of individuals in a test population that dies from 50 mg of the chemical
(D) The dose that kills 50 individuals in a test population
(E) The dose that kills 50% of a test population

58. The Law of Competitive Exclusion states that:

(A) Interspecific competition is harmful in ecosystems
(B) Intraspecific competition is harmful in ecosystems
(C) Two species in the same ecosystem can always occupy the same ecological niche
(D) Two species in the same ecosystem cannot occupy the same ecological niche
(E) Individuals only compete for resources with members of the same species

Questions 59-61 refer to the graph below, which represents changes in temperature as altitude increases in the atmosphere.

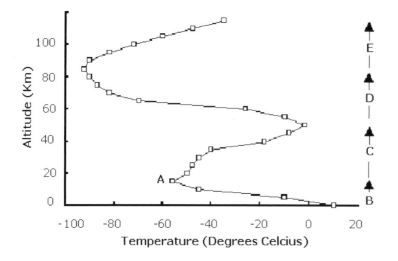

59. Represents the atmospheric layer that contains helpful ozone

60. Represents the tropopause

61. Represents the atmospheric layer made up of ionized gases heated by solar energy; this layer also contains the aurora borealis

62. What is the most commonly used measure of a country's economic growth?

(A) Replacement level fertility
(B) Gross National Product (GNP)
(C) Human Development Index (HDI)
(D) Externalized costs
(E) Natality rate

63. According to the National Environmental Policy Act (NEPA), every government agency must file a(n) _____ before carrying out a major federal project that could affect the environment

(A) Declaration of bioremediation
(B) Environmental impact statement
(C) Cost-benefit analysis
(D) Biogeographical report
(E) Statement of environmental alternatives

64. What irrigation technique used for agriculture results in the least amount of water lost to evaporation?

(A) Laser-level irrigation
(B) Gravity-flow irrigation
(C) Flood irrigation
(D) Drip irrigation
(E) Sprinklers

65. Which of the following best characterizes the soil in the tropical moist forest biome?

(A) Thin, acidic, and nutrient-poor
(B) Thick and nutrient-rich
(C) Considered the richest farmland in the world
(D) Similar to that of grasslands
(E) Usually includes a hardpan layer

66. Which of the following is the most abundant element in the Earth's core?

(A) Phosphorus
(B) Nitrogen
(C) Carbon
(D) Oxygen
(E) Iron

67. During what two seasons does the thermocline of a freshwater lake disappear due to seasonal turnover?

(A) Summer and Winter
(B) Summer and Autumn
(C) Autumn and Spring
(D) Summer and Spring
(E) Autumn and Winter

68. Which of the following is an environmental problem associated with using heap-leach extraction to separate pure metals from ore?

(A) Cyanide may contaminate groundwater
(B) The extraction process may lead to massive fires and explosions
(C) Extraction sites may be abandoned
(D) Both A and C
(E) None of the above

69. Many bird species reduce competition by feeding at different levels and on different parts of trees. This behavior is best described as:

(A) Critical factors
(B) Tolerance limits
(C) Resource partitioning
(D) Territoriality
(E) Batesian mimicry

70. The relationship between epiphytes and the trees on which they grow is an example of what concept?

(A) Mutualism
(B) Commensalism
(C) Parasitism
(D) Coevolution
(E) Host specific interaction

71. Humus is responsible for all of the following characteristics of soil EXCEPT:

(A) Gives soil its structure
(B) Increases organic content
(C) Increases water absorption
(D) Increases nutrient-holding capacity

99

(E) Prevents soil particles from sticking together

72. What is the primary fuel used in the nuclear reactions of a Pressurized-Water Reactor (PWR)?

(A) U-235
(B) U-238
(C) U-239
(D) Plutonium 239
(E) Uranium ore

73. The bottom stratum of a lake that is low in dissolved oxygen but contains high levels of nutrients from sinking detritus is called the:

(A) Limnetic zone
(B) Littoral zone
(C) Epilimnion
(D) Benthos layer
(E) Hypolimnion

74. Which of the following is NOT a method preferred in the US for the treatment of hazardous waste?

(A) Placement in permanent retrievable storage
(B) Placement in a secure landfill
(C) Bioremediation
(D) Incineration
(E) Recycling

75. A major source of radon contamination in US houses is _____, which has been connected to _____

(A) Paint; lung cancer
(B) Atmospheric inversions; skin cancer
(C) The underlying bedrock; lung cancer
(D) Tropospheric ozone; neurological disorders
(E) Combustion of biomass; immune dysfunctions

76. What is the function of photovoltaic cells?

(A) To capture solar energy and directly convert it to an electric current
(B) To focus and redirect solar energy onto water-carrying pipes
(C) To absorb tremendous amounts of solar heat for storage
(D) To reduce nitrogen-oxide emissions from automobiles
(E) To increase photosynthetic rate by administering electric shock to green plants

77. Which of the following is/are advantages of using biomass as a primary fuel source?

I. It emits less SO_2 than conventional fuel sources
II. It is not time-consuming
III. It releases insignificant quantities of particulate matter
IV. It reduces populations of bioinvasive species

(A) I only

(B) IV only
(C) I and III only
(D) I and IV only
(E) I, II, III, and IV

78. Replacement level fertility is:

(A) A little less than 2
(B) A little more than 2
(C) 3
(D) A little more than 3
(E) 15

79. What country has the largest supply of proven oil reserves?

(A) Japan
(B) China
(C) Saudi Arabia
(D) Iraq
(E) Russia

80. The giant saguaro cactus, which grows in the hot Sonoran desert, is extremely sensitive to low temperatures. In fact, an exceptionally cold winter night can kill growing tips on branches. In this case, temperature is an example of a(n):

(A) Intolerance factor
(B) Sensitivity gauge
(C) Physiological stress limit
(D) Specialist factor
(E) Critical limiting factor

81. In a fire-climax community, fire is important in fulfilling which of the following functions?

(A) Returning nutrients to the soil
(B) Maintaining plant populations by preventing seeds from germinating
(C) Clearing dead plant material
(D) Both A and B
(E) Both A and C

82. Researchers have observed that when toxins in asbestos react with toxins in cigarette smoke, their cumulative toxicity is greater than the sum of the individual toxins. Asbestos and cigarette smoke are therefore considered:

(A) Additive toxins
(B) Antagonistic toxins
(C) Synergistic toxins
(D) Polar toxins
(E) Covalent toxins

83. The Clean Water Act requires that the _____ be used to clean up point sources, while the _____ be used to clean up toxins

(A) Best Practicable Technology; Best Available Technology
(B) Best Available Technology; Best Practicable Technology
(C) Minimum Daily Load; Maximum Daily Load

(D) Maximum Daily Load; Minimum Daily Load
(E) EPA; WHO

84. Certain tropical figs, which bear during seasons when no other fruit is available, play essential roles in their ecosystems. When these tropical fig plants are removed, many animals would starve along with the other plant species that depend on them, causing the ecosystem to fall apart. Based on this information, the tropical fig plant is an example of a(n):

(A) Generalist
(B) K-selected species
(C) r-selected species
(D) Keystone species
(E) Specialist

85. Why do exotic species usually become pests?

(A) They proliferate quickly, since they lack natural predators
(B) They increase biodiversity
(C) They have low biotic potential
(D) A and B
(E) A, B, and C

86. Which of the following is NOT an example of a nonrenewable resource?

(A) Soil
(B) Oil
(C) Minerals
(D) Metals
(E) Coal

87. Reliable wind patterns such as the westerlies and trade winds are created and shaped by what factor(s)?

(A) The Coriolis Effect
(B) Uneven solar heating
(C) Differences in temperature and pressure
(D) All of the above
(E) None of the above

88. The goal of ecological economics is to create a steady-state economy characterized by all of the following EXCEPT:

(A) Recycling of materials
(B) Low birth and death rates
(C) Emphasis on efficiency
(D) Emphasis on durability of goods
(E) All of the above are characteristics of a steady-state economy

89. The giant panda feeds exclusively on bamboo and can tolerate a narrow range of environmental conditions. Based on this information, the giant panda has a _____ niche
(A) Fundamental
(B) Realized
(C) Specialist

(D) Generalist
(E) Detritivore

90. Until recently, most superfund money came from what source?

(A) Taxes on the general public
(B) Taxes on producers of toxic and hazardous wastes
(C) Taxes on automobile manufacturers
(D) Budgetary funds cut from other federal agencies
(E) Donations by environmental concern groups

91. A certain radioactive substance has a half-life of 20 years. What percent of the original sample will *remain* after 40 years?

(A) 75%
(B) 65%
(C) 50%
(D) 30%
(E) 25%

92. Which of the following is NOT an argument used by environmentalists against increased petroleum exploration in the arctic?

(A) Machinery emissions would cause an overall decrease in temperature in the region
(B) Vegetation would be damaged by deposition of alkaline dust along roads
(C) Habitat would be destroyed by gravel roads
(D) Oils spills would contaminate soil and water
(E) Machinery emissions would contribute to acid rain

93. Benefits of recycling include:

I. Recycling usually does not require an initial investment
II. Recycled products are very popular
III. Recycling saves raw materials
IV. Recycling does not require construction of special facilities

(A) I only
(B) II only
(C) III only
(D) I and III only
(E) I, III, and IV

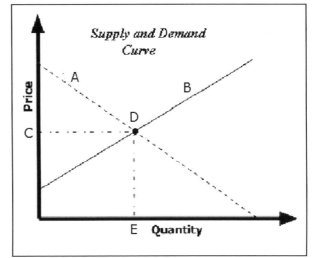

Questions 94-95 refer to the supply and demand curve pictured (right).

94. Represents the amount of product that consumers will buy

95. Represents market equilibrium

96. What is the greatest source of freshwater for humans worldwide?

(A) Atmosphere
(B) Groundwater
(C) Glaciers
(D) Rivers
(E) Lakes

97. In the process of cloud seeding, particulates are sprayed into the air to encourage rain. In this case, the particulates serve as _____

(A) Rain shadows
(B) Condensation nuclei
(C) Dew points
(D) Humidity nuclei
(E) Saturation points

98. Unlike that of the Neo-Marxists, the main argument of the Neo-Malthusians is that:

(A) The human population should be stabilized through social justice
(B) Technology has increased the world's carrying capacity for humans
(C) The human population should be stabilized through birth control
(D) Countries above the Brandt Line should share their wealth with developing countries
(E) A larger population means a larger workforce and a better economy

99. The combustion of one gallon of gasoline creates approximately 5 lbs of CO_2. If an automobile gets 20 miles to the gallon, how much CO_2 will be released on a 400-mile drive?

(A) 20 lbs
(B) 40 lbs
(C) 60 lbs
(D) 80 lbs
(E) 100 lbs

100. The process of smelting separates pure metals from ore by:

(A) Heating the ore to high temperatures
(B) Dissolving the ore using cyanide
(C) Exposing the ore to calcium carbonate
(D) Physically chipping away the surrounding rock
(E) Heap-leach extraction

STOP! Take a 10 min break before continuing to the free-response section of the exam.

ENVIRONMENTAL SCIENCE
Section II
4 Questions
Time – 1 hour and 30 minutes
No Calculators!

Directions: All four questions are weighted equally. The suggested time is about 22 minutes for answering each question. On the actual exam, you will be writing your answers in a pink booklet. Where explanation or discussion is required, support your answers with relevant information and/or specific examples.

1. Read the article below and answer the questions that follow.

China's Three Gorges Dam Completed

After a decade of work, China has finally filled the reservoir for the Three Gorges Dam, the most colossal hydroelectric project in history, allowing the flood-prone Yangtze River to create a 600 km reservoir. China claims that the $25 billion dam is necessary to tame the Yangtze, whose floods are a major cause of death in the region. Government authorities assert that energy from the dam will also help to meet future energy demand and begin generating much-needed power for the booming Chinese economy.

---

   a) Discuss TWO ecological problems and ONE social or economic problem associated with the construction and/or use of large dams.

   b) Besides diverting water for urban consumption, identify and briefly describe an alternative technique (that does not involve dams) to increase the water supply in a dry region.

   c) Groundwater is currently the greatest source of freshwater for humans. Explain TWO negative consequences of excess groundwater withdrawal.

2. The data below regards the heating of a cabin in the United States. Use the data to answer the questions that follow.

     ■ One pound of coal supplies 10,000 BTUs of heat energy
     ■ The furnace is 80% efficient
     ■ The cabin is 1000 square feet
     ■ 60,000 BTUs of heat per square foot are required to heat the cabin this season
     ■ Coal costs $8 per pound

   a) Do the following calculations. Show every step and include units in your answer.
   (i) How much coal is needed to heat the cabin this season?

   (ii) How much will it cost to heat the cabin this season?

b) Identify one action the campers can take to lower this cost by conserving heat energy.

c) Choose TWO criteria air pollutants released during the combustion of coal. For each criteria pollutant, discuss any environmental crises or health problems with which it is associated.

d) Describe an alternative source of energy that can be used to heat the cabin, categorize it as renewable or nonrenewable, and explain any pros or cons with which it is associated.

3. Answer the following questions concerning pesticide use:

a) Explain the environmental effects of excessive use of DDT. What effect did it have on predatory birds and why?

b) Discuss the pesticide treadmill and the mechanisms through which it occurs.

c) Describe TWO benefits to pesticide-use. Describe TWO alternatives to pesticide-use.

4. Answer the following questions concerning the biogeochemical cycles:

a) Explain the Nitrogen Cycle. Draw a diagram to clarify your points.

b) How have humans impacted the Nitrogen Cycle? Explain cultural eutrophication and how it occurs.

c) Explain the Carbon Cycle. Draw a diagram to clarify your points.

d) Human activities have increased the amount of carbon dioxide in the atmosphere, impacting the Carbon Cycle and causing global warming. Assess TWO possible effects of global warming due to excess carbon dioxide.

GRADING YOUR PRACTICE TEST

Multiple-Choice Section

Calculate your raw score using the following formula:

Number correct (out of 100): A. _____

Number Wrong (out of 100): B. _____

Weighted Score on Multiple-Choice = (A) – (¼)(B) = _____

Free-Response Section

Compare your answers to the overview of the free-response on the upcoming pages. Give yourself a score from 0 (blank) to 10 (perfect) on each question.

Score on Question 1: _____ x 1.5 = C. _____

Score on Question 2: _____ x 1.5 = D. _____

Score on Question 3: _____ x 1.5 = E. _____

Score on Question 4: _____ x 1.5 = F. _____

Weighted Score on Free-Response = C + D + E + F = _____

Composite Score

Composite Score =
Multiple-Choice Weighted Score + Free-Response Weighted Score = _____

To obtain your AP Grade, compare your Composite Score to the following chart:

Composite Score	AP Grade
120-160	5
94-119	4
68-93	3
38-67	2
0-37	1

ANSWER KEY: MULTIPLE-CHOICE

1.	D	51.	A
2.	E	52.	E
3.	C	53.	C
4.	B	54.	D
5.	C	55.	B
6.	A	56.	A
7.	B	57.	E
8.	D	58.	D
9.	B	59.	C
10.	C	60.	A
11.	C	61.	E
12.	D	62.	B
13.	A	63.	B
14.	B	64.	D
15.	E	65.	A
16.	B	66.	E
17.	D	67.	C
18.	E	68.	D
19.	B	69.	C
20.	A	70.	B
21.	D	71.	E
22.	B	72.	A
23.	A	73.	D
24.	E	74.	D
25.	B	75.	C
26.	C	76.	A
27.	A	77.	D
28.	D	78.	B
29.	C	79.	C
30.	B	80.	E
31.	A	81.	E
32.	D	82.	C
33.	E	83.	B
34.	E	84.	D
35.	B	85.	A
36.	C	86.	A
37.	A	87.	D
38.	D	88.	E
39.	E	89.	C
40.	D	90.	B
41.	B	91.	E
42.	C	92.	A
43.	C	93.	C
44.	E	94.	A
45.	A	95.	D
46.	B	96.	B
47.	D	97.	B
48.	B	98.	C
49.	C	99.	E
50.	E	100.	A

EXPLANATIONS: MULTIPLE-CHOICE

1-4. See Pg. 65 about wastewater treatment

5-9. See Pg. 56 about air pollutants

10. Love Canal was the former toxic waste dumpsite that was converted to an elementary school, causing serious illnesses in neighborhood residents.

11. The Kyoto Protocol is an international agreement to reduce greenhouse gas emissions, which are linked to global warming.

12. This one's a little tricky... you have to use the equation for doubling time. The time it takes for a population to double equals 70 divided by % annual growth. In this case, it equals 70/7, or 10 years for the population to double. This means that in 10 years, the population will be 100 million. In 20 years, the population will double twice, making it equal 200 million.

13. This fact about sanitary landfills was stated on Pg. 67.

14. In parasitism, one member benefits (tapeworm) and the other is harmed (human).

15. This fact about biomes was stated on Pg. 26.

16. This fact was stated on Pg. 19

17. The populations size doesn't matter, it's just there to confuse you. Use the doubling time equation: 70/3.5 = 20 years.

18. See Pg. 53. Nitrogen (N_2) makes up more than three-quarters of the atmosphere.

19. See Pg. 12.

20. Photosynthesis uses up carbon dioxide and results in oxygen. See Pg. 11.

21. See Pg. 19. CITES stands for Convention on International Trade in Endangered Species.

22. In demographic transition, death rate is first decreased (A), followed by a decrease in birth rate (D), causing the population to stabilize (C). This puts resources under control, and leads to a more developed country (E). The only choice left is (B).

23. The "not" in choice (B) makes it incorrect. Hardin argues that resources will be degraded if everyone is given unregulated access. Instead, individuals should feel responsibility towards their resources. See Pg. 41.

24. The pesticide treadmill occurs because excessive pesticide-use allows only the naturally pesticide-resistant organisms to survive, which subsequently pass on these traits to their offspring. The same process occurs with antibiotic-resistant bacteria. Natural selection over the generations has also favored polar bears with

camouflaging fur, which are most "fit" to survive. The Galapagos Finches evolved different beaks through natural selection to become best adapted to certain food sources on the various islands.

25. See Pg. 26. Permafrost is only found in the Tundra.

26. Cultural eutrophication, discussed on Pg. 64, leads to algal blooms. Since algae use up available oxygen, eutrophication leads to a hypoxic zone and a *reduction* in dissolved oxygen. The algae also make the water appear murky.

27. Review the biogeochemical cycles starting on Pg. 15.

28. See Pg. 32

29. The biotic potential is the maximum rate of reproduction for a species, so it should be the steepest part of the graph.

30. The logistic growth model has an S-shape.

31. See pie graph on Pg. 70.

32. Herbivores cannot produce their own food, so they're not producers. They are primary consumers because they eat plants.

33. Review plate tectonics, Pg. 50.

34. Nonpoint sources, like runoff, have no specific location where they discharge into a body of water.

35. Review biogeochemical cycles starting on Pg. 15.

36. Desertification is associated with land degradation, especially through overgrazing. It has nothing to do with dams.

37. See Pg. 63. BOD and DO are inversely related. This leaves either (A) or (B) as possible answers. Downstream from a pollutant, BOD increases because microorganisms start decomposing the pollutants. The microorganisms take in oxygen, causing DO levels to decrease.

38. See Pg. 33.

39. See Pg. 50.

40. Pg. 44 reviews the soil horizons.

41. DDT became increasingly concentrated as it went up the food chain, so it biomagnified. In predatory birds, it interfered with calcium deposition, making their egg shells break easily.

42. Since algal blooms are unrelated to groundwater depletion, eliminate choice (D). Acidification relates to sulfur dioxide, not to groundwater depletion. This leaves only I and IV.

43. Erosion actually *reduces* crop production by carrying away valuable topsoil.

44. The Precautionary Principle basically states that it's better to be safe than sorry. This corresponds to choice (E).

45. See Pg. 49.

46. See Pg. 72 to review the parts and functions in a nuclear power plant.

47. Coliform Bacteria are found in the gut of animals, and they are released in animal waste. They indicate that there is untreated waste in the water, and correspond with infectious agents.

48. This fact was stated on Pg. 45.

49. Primary succession occurs in an area that did not previously support life.

50. See Pg. 51.

51. Wetlands have nothing to do with introduced, or exotic species.

52. If you know one of the blanks, use it to cross off incorrect answer choices, leaving only the correct one. Also eliminate obvious wrong answers like the London Dumping Convention. See Pg. 79.

53. Emergent diseases are recently *emerging* into the human population.

54. Urban sprawl is covered on Pg. 37.

55. See Pg. 11.

56. This is the Ten percent rule covered on Pg. 13.

57. LD50 stands for lethal dose, 50%, which is the dose that kills off 50% of a test population.

58. See Pg. 22.

59-61. Review graph on Pg. 53. The stratosphere contains good ozone, while the thermosphere is made up of ionized gases.

62. This fact was stated on Pg. 41.

63. See Pg. 43.

64. Drip irrigation reduces evaporation because it delivers a small quantity of water directly to the crop.

65. See Pg. 28.

66. See Pg. 50.

67. During autumn and spring, air temperatures begin to change, causing the water in a lake to mix. The thermocline then disappears.

68. See Pg. 52 about heap-leach extraction.

69. Resource partitioning involves splitting up resources so that two species do not occupy exactly the same niche.

111

70. In commensalisms, one species benefits (the epiphyte gains increased sunlight), while the other (tree) remains unharmed.

71. See Pg. 44.

72. See Pg. 71 about fission in a nuclear power plant.

73. The benthos layer is the lake bottom.

74. Hazardous waste should not be incinerated, or burned, because it may release harmful substances into the air.

75. This fact was stated on Pg. 57.

76. Use the structure of the word: "photo" means light and "voltaic" relates to electricity.

77. Gathering wood takes up most of the day in developing countries, while burning it can release soot and other particulates.

78. Replacement level fertility is having only enough children to replace the parents. It is a little more than 2 to make up for infant mortality.

79. Saudi Arabia has 25% of proven oil reserves.

80. See Pg. 23.

81. Fire actually *helps* seeds germinate in fire-climax communities, for instance, by melting sap in cones and releasing seeds. Fire burns away dead shrubs, while the ash returns nutrients to the soil.

82. Synergistic toxins have a greater cumulative toxicity than their individual sums.

83. See Pg. 64.

84. See Pg. 24.

85. Exotic species tend to have *high* biotic potential because they reproduce rapidly. Moreover, they *decrease* biodiversity because they take over an area, smothering out other, native species.

86. Something that is NOT a nonrenewable resource *is* a renewable resource. Be careful when you're reading the question.

87. See Pg. 54 for factors that affect wind patterns.

88. See Pg. 40.

89. Specialists, like the giant panda, tolerate a small range of environmental factors. In fact, many are endangered for that reason.

90. The revolving funds for CERCLA, or the Superfund Act, came from a tax on the factories and corporations that produced the hazardous waste.

91. This is another tricky one! Imagine that you start with 100 grams of an isotope. After 20 years, half of it, 50 grams, will remain. After 40 years, half of that, or 25 grams, will remain. If you have 25 grams and you started with 100 grams, only 25% of the original isotope remains. You can plug in your own numbers any time the question asks for a percent.

92. See Pg. 47.

93. See Pg. 68 about the pros and cons of recycling.

94. The amount of products a consumer will buy is the demand.

95. Market equilibrium is where the supply and demand curves intersect.

96. See Pg. 60.

97. The particulates provide a surface onto which water vapor can accumulate and condense into water droplets. Therefore, cloud seeding uses the concept of condensation nuclei.

98. Neo-Malthusians agree with Malthus about stabilizing the human population. They believe that the best way to do so is through birth control.

99. For each gallon, the car can drive 20 miles. Therefore, a 400 mile drive will use up 400/20, or 20 gallons of gas. If combustion of 1 gallon releases 5 lbs of CO_2, then combustion of 20 gallons will release $(20)*(5)$, or 100 lbs of CO_2.

100. Look at the word "smelting"… included is the word "melting". Smelting involves heating an ore at high temperatures, essentially melting it, to extract pure metal.

FREE-RESPONSE RUBRIC

1.
a) **1 pt** for description of each ecological problem (maximum **2 pts**). Explanation of any two of the following in sufficient:

- Loss of free-flowing rivers
- Disruption of fish migrations
- Ecosystem losses, since large dams collect silt and increase turbidity upstream and starve streambeds downstream
- Waste of water due to evaporation and seepage into porous rock beds

2 pts for description of a social/economic problem. Explanation of any of the following in sufficient:

- Rise in water levels floods towns and farmlands
- Displacement of people from homes
- Loss of historic artifacts and economic losses from property damage when cities are submerged

b) **2 pts** for identification and explanation of any of the following techniques to bring water to dry region:

- Cloud seeding
- Desalinization
- Tow an iceberg
- Transfer water from elsewhere

c) **2 pts** for description of **each** negative consequence of excess water withdrawal (maximum **4 pts**). Explanation of any two of the following is sufficient:

- Dry spells of rivers and streams, since many surface waters use groundwater to recharge
- Salinization of soil and aquifers
- Subsidence
- Sinkholes
- Cones of depression and collapse of aquifers

2.
a) (i) 1000 ft^2 x $\dfrac{60,000 \text{ BTUs}}{\text{ft}^2}$ x $\dfrac{1 \text{ lb}}{10,000 \text{ BTUs}}$ = 6000 lbs of coal

However, you must also take into account the efficiency of the furnace:

.8 (c) = 6000 ← 80% of the total amount needed equals 6000

c = | 7500 lbs of coal | **3 pts for correct answer and work**

(ii) 7500 lbs x $\dfrac{\$8}{\text{lb}}$ = | $600 | **1 pt for correct answer and work**

114

b) **1 pt** for identification and **1 pt** for elaboration. Explanation of any of the following actions (or similar ones) is sufficient:

- Increase efficiency of furnace
- Improve insulation through use of curtains or double-paned windows, weather-stripping for heat escape, etc.
- Use blankets indoors instead of thermostat
- Utilize passive solar heat, for instance, by making larger windows

c) **1 pt** for *each* criteria pollutant and **1 pt** for *each* environmental crisis/health issue (maximum of **4 pts**). Any of the following is sufficient:

- Sulfur dioxide: acid deposition
- Carbon monoxide: inhibits human respiration by binding to hemoglobin, preventing oxygen uptake; cause of many deaths. Also a greenhouse gas linked to global warming.
- Particulate material (soot, ash): reduces visibility, damages lung tissue
- Nitrogen oxides: photochemical smog, acid deposition

3.
a) **1 pt** for description of one or more of the following environmental/health effects of DDT:

- Biomagnification and disruption of non-target species
- Pest resurgence through pesticide resistance or killing of natural predators
- Creation of new pests through killing of natural predators
- Human health: acute poisoning, cancer, birth defects, immune problems, chronic degenerative diseases

1 pt for identification of effect on predatory birds:

- Many, such as the Brown Pelican, became endangered and their populations drastically dropped.

1 pt for explanation of effect on predatory birds:

- DDT interfered with calcium deposition, making their egg shells thin and brittle, so that they easily broke

b) **1 pt** for definition of pesticide treadmill: a need for new or constantly increasing doses of pesticides to prevent pest resurgence

2 pts for explanation of pesticide resistance and concept of natural selection as it relates to this concept. There is genetic variation among pest populations. During a treatment with pesticides, only the pests that are naturally resistant to pesticides survive, passing on the trait for resistance to their offspring and eventually creating a resistant population.

c) **1 pt** for *each* benefit and explanation; **1 pt** for *each* alternative and explanation (Maximum **4 pts**). For pesticide benefits, explanation of two of the following is sufficient:

- Disease control, as with malaria
- Increased crop yield by preventing crop diseases
- Increased crop yield by reducing insect predation

- Increased crop production by reducing competition from weeds

For pesticide alternatives, explanation of any two of the following is sufficient:

- Alter agricultural practices to reduce insects and weeds; for example, cover crop, crop rotation, switching from monoculture to mixed polyculture, etc.
- Biological controls: introduce predator or pathogen
- Integrated Pest Management
- Introduce sterile males into pest population

4.

a) **2 pts** for explanation of Nitrogen Cycle; **1 pt** for diagram. See Pg 16.

b) **1 pt** for human impact on Nitrogen Cycle: through the creation of nitrogen-containing fertilizers.

   1 pt for definition and causes of cultural eutrophication:

- Eutrophication is caused by excess plant nutrients in surface water, particularly nitrates and phosphates, which result in algal blooms.
- Eutrophication is when the resulting algal blooms reduce water clarity and oxygen levels.

c) **2 pts** for explanation of Carbon Cycle; **1 pt** for diagram. See Pg 15.

d) **1 pt** for *each* description of possible effect of global warming (maximum **2 pts**). Explanation of any two of the following is sufficient:

- Rise in temperatures makes sea ice and alpine glaciers recede, increasing water level and destroying habitat
- Reduce biodiversity because temperatures surpass range of tolerance for many species
- Change in ocean circulation, leading to severe storms
- Warm temperatures proliferate rodents and insects that carry disease
- Higher temperatures melt permafrost in tundra, releasing methane

ABOUT THE AUTHOR

At the time she wrote this book, Michelle Mahanian was an undergraduate attending the University of California, Los Angeles (UCLA) on full academic scholarship. While in high school, Michelle completed a total of ten Advanced Placement (AP) courses with a score of 5 on every AP exam. Consequently, the College Board has honored her as a National AP Scholar. Michelle's first-hand experience with the AP program has given her the personal insight necessary to author a study aid of high caliber. An experienced tutor, she is founder of Smartypants Publishing™. Moreover, Michelle has been recognized by Harvard University, The University of Rochester, Cornell University, and Johns Hopkins University for her scholastic achievements.

Made in the USA
Middletown, DE
18 March 2016